To
Dr Reyes,

Thank you for your
wonderful hospitality.

We walk out of an

evening like

'damp velvet'!

Here's looking at

you!

Tim Steele

The End of Politics: Triangulation, Realignment and the Battle for the Centre Ground

The End of Politics

Triangulation, Realignment and the Battle for the Centre Ground

Alexander Lee and Timothy Stanley

POLITICO'S

First published in Great Britain 2006 by
Politico's Publishing Ltd, an imprint of
Methuen Publishing Ltd
11–12 Buckingham Gate
London
SW1E 6LB

10 9 8 7 6 5 4 3 2 1

A CIP catalogue record for this book is available from the British Library.

ISBN-10: 1-84275-174-3
ISBN-13: 978-1-84275-174-9

Typeset by SX Composing DTP, Rayleigh, Essex
Printed and bound in Great Britain by The Cromwell Press, Trowbridge, Wiltshire

Contents

Preface and acknowledgments

Change is an inevitable feature of politics. As time goes on, circumstances alter, policies are revised and the electorate casts its votes in new ways. Although the most recent developments might stimulate some flurry of activity in the corridors of Westminster or some controversy in the studios of television stations, there is seldom a sense of bewilderment and uncertainty accompanying political change. The spring of 2006, however, seems to have left commentators and politicians deeply unsettled. In mid-April, a report was published by the Joseph Rowntree Reform Trust which suggested that in the forthcoming local elections, a quarter of the voters in London were considering voting for the British National Party (BNP). Following BNP candidates on the campaign trail in Dagenham, the *Spectator* reported that almost half of the voters approached reacted favourably to the party's far-right-wing policies. A study by the *Daily Telegraph* indicated that the far right was winning support in equal measures from all three mainstream parties, and not just amongst the disgruntled, urban working class. Voter anger and historically unique levels of support for the BNP have presented politicians and commentators alike with a distinct paradox. How could it be that so abhorrent a political party was able to attract so positive a response among ordinary voters, often living in areas which in previous years had displayed a marked predisposition to vote for Labour, the Conservatives or the Liberal Democrats? Why was it that those from the major parties' traditional social constituencies were beginning to abandon their earlier political allegiances on such a striking scale?

Explanations ranged from the sublime to the ridiculous, but behind each there was a sense that the very terms of British political debate were shifting in a new and unforeseen fashion. At the same time as public figures were desperately trying to understand the sudden growth of support for the BNP, journalists began to talk with increasing concern of 'the end of ideology'. Opinion pieces have started to argue – for the first time – that mainstream political discourse has become so fixated on the pursuit of the 'centre ground' that it has jettisoned the discussion of ideological principles. Writing for the BBC, Bob Tyrrell claimed that Labour, the Conservatives and the Liberal Democrats had shed their ideological mantles and pondered with uncertainty what the future might hold in store. The comment pages of newspapers and, increasingly, the speeches of Parliament and stump have betrayed a growing awareness of a paradigm change and, in their tone and tenor, communicated a deep sense of discomfort and loss.

Whilst many have argued the case for a profound alteration in British politics, no serious attempt was made to understand its nature, or to comprehend its causes and effects. Frequently, efforts were constrained by the short-term interests of daily editions and hourly bulletins, or compromised by immediate party-political interests. We believe that this quiet revolution first began in earnest in the 2005 general election and that the rise of protest politics and voting is indicative of a change in our political discourse affected by the mainstream parties themselves. As political activists we began to detect that our generation stands at a crossroads between one variety of politics and another, and we decided to draw together electoral analyses and political debate to better understand this fundamental shift taking place. Our findings – the result of painstaking research over several months – were far more shocking than we had expected and, presenting us with a clearer idea of the subtle, yet seismic changes to our political order which have already occurred, compelled us to reassess the very basis of our own political beliefs. Since the first draft of this book was completed in the early months of 2006, the questions we asked ourselves have become more pressing and the possibilities which initially concerned us have become concrete realities.

As this study of the state of modern British politics has forced us to reconsider every aspect of our political beliefs, so we hope that it will challenge the reader's assumptions and provoke a wider debate about the very function of politics in the twenty-first century.

★

The authors would like to thank Alan Gordon Walker, Jonathan Wadman, Catherine Bailey and the staff of Politico's for all the effort that has gone into producing this book. We would also like to express our gratitude to the Faculty of History at the University of Cambridge and to the School of History and Classics at the University of Edinburgh. Finally, sincere thanks must go to James O'Connor for all the help that he has given the authors during the writing of this book.

Introduction

Released in 1995, Mathieu Kassovitz's film *La Haine* depicted a France torn apart by racial and cultural conflict. In a capital city that prides itself on its Enlightenment traditions of egality and brotherhood, the film documented the breakdown of civil society amidst ethnic violence. Specifically it followed a night in the life of three French boys of Jewish, Arabic and African descent as they try to make their way through a riot-torn city. The revolutionary state was depicted as eating its children, in a bleak landscape of deserted and lurid shopping malls, immigrant slums and sporadic police violence. The film divided the French public; police demonstrated outside cinemas and the Cabinet requested a private screening. The screening itself is significant for the argument of this book because it implies that the French government felt dislocated from the growing underclass within its own society. In particular they could not immediately empathise with the experience of the migrant communities: a fictional feature film had been elevated to the status of documentary.

This degree of self-assessment and honesty on the part of the Cabinet reflected the fact that the French political system has always been under-prepared for the tasks of assimilation, despite having a national culture based not upon race or religion but upon secularism and humanistic ideology. The brand of corporatist nationalism espoused by de Gaulle and his successors on the right has always been guilty of intense national chauvinism, while on the left the French Socialist Party's doctrinaire attitude towards politics has made it insensitive to non–class-based conflicts. For instance, during the early stages of the Algerian war for independence it fervently supported the French colonial authority in the hope that it might integrate the Arab proletariat into its own. *La Haine* was produced at the end of the Mitterrand government, an administration that had largely derailed the French socialist experiment, leaving a greater degree of political realignment in its wake. After a period of flirtation with socialist economics France's first leftist President had redirected the economy towards European integration and the free market. Crises of confidence in socialism after the fall of the Berlin Wall and in the apparently endemic corruption within corporatist Gaullism were reflected not only in ethnic violence but also in the reinvigoration of the communist movement, a buoyant nationalist right and the beginnings of libertarianism amongst centrist conservatives. The latter has been championed by Nicolas Sarkozy, current minister for the interior, figurehead of the politics of *libéralisme* and potentially the next President. In short, France's twentieth-century traditional mainstream parties are proving tragically underprepared for the political challenges of the next decade. *La Haine* is evidence of dislocation amongst French voters, a failure to identify with national values and the growth of problems and sectional interests no longer defined easily in post-war language. The French Cabinet's willingness to learn from it is proof of the existence of a barrier between the French state and its people, a crisis of both communication and political structure. In 1995 the government was faced with a range of new economic and social problems. It felt not only ill equipped to deal with them but incapable of communicating with their protagonists.

This book is largely a reflection upon the state of British politics, but by starting in France it should be apparent that what it seeks to study is an international phenomenon. Each country has responded differently to its changing political landscapes, depending upon culture, wealth, demography and accident. But all Western democracies are going through a period of profound change. There is taking place a slow and unsure readjustment under the pressure of a New Politics. This New Politics is characterised in part by physical changes to the context within which democracies function. Economies are becoming fluid, global and electric. Computers and telecommunications have significantly altered people's relations with the world around them. Like old soldiers, primary industries have faded away or gone abroad to work for someone else. But what interests this study is a corresponding political shift in language, identity and ideology. The discourse of left versus right, defined by the socialist–capitalist confrontation of the last century, is becoming antiquated and almost anachronistic. A plethora of new discourses is emerging. They include environmentalism, ethnic conflict, fair and free trade, sexuality, gender and the right to hunt. Moreover, the needs of the new voters, those who do not readily identify themselves with twentieth-century political labels, are breaking down traditional electoral coalitions. This pattern is perhaps more dramatically apparent abroad, for instance in the rise of civil disobedience in Europe or the defection of blue-collar Democrats to the Republicans in America. But there is evidence too that voters at home feel under-represented. Circumstances are different, policy choices radically so. But through our own methods and mistakes, all historically unique to Britain though not beyond comparison with other Western democracies, we are reaching a point at which our mainstream parties are failing to convince the public of the value of engaging in party politics, and in some cases in engaging in politics at all. Parties are losing their loyalties among their traditional voting blocs. They are losing ideological cohesion. They are losing activists. They are losing the ability to analyse and correct mistakes of policy. Most importantly of all, they are losing the public's attention and affection. The violent dis-engagement of ethnic minorities in France from the political process is a visceral example of frustration with a political system that fails to provide adequate representation. It is our contention that such a disengagement is taking place on a broader, subtler level in British society today.

A much overlooked survey took place after the 2001 election that studied this disengagement from parliamentary politics in fine detail. Robert Worcester and Roger Mortimore's *Explaining Labour's Second Landslide* contained an adroit section on apathy. Contrary to popular theory the British public is not uninterested in politics. It does not even subscribe to as wholeheartedly cynical a view of politicians' morality and motivation as one might suspect. Indeed trust in government ministers' opinions has grown, if only marginally, since the early 1990s. According to our findings only 14 per cent of the electorate trusted politicians to tell the truth 'most of the time' in 1993: a figure that subsequently peaked at 23 per cent in 1999 and then hovered around

20 per cent in the years running up to the invasion of Iraq. Worcester and Mortimore determined that 'the public's interest in politics has remained very stable over the past three decades, suggesting that people are no more "turned-off" by politics per se than they were in the past'. But they did discover that 'the 2001 election did not connect with people and made them view it differently to previous ones. Certainly it seems it was more short-term factors than a long-term decline that were the immediate cause of the fall in turnout.' The evidence was convincing. Their surveys found that a vast majority of electors still vote for 'positive' reasons linked with 'civic duty' and the recognition that not voting denies a person's right to complain. Indeed the public demonstrated in 2001 an ingrained and almost regimented loyalty towards the democratic process. Of those who trudged out to vote, some 68 per cent had 'little or no interest' in the actual result. The vast majority of respondents disagreed that voting did not have an impact upon their lives and it was notable that the young were only marginally more apathetic than those in their autumnal years. This was despite the fact that only 30 per cent regarded the election as interesting, while an enormous 66 per cent found it to be a bit of a drag. The large number of those who stayed at home hid an even larger figure of those who voted but were unconcerned by the result.

We found that the British people are still political animals but that they consider their views to be ill reflected by the major parties. Most importantly, their response has been disengagement from association with, and political activism within, those very parties. Instead they are increasingly aligning themselves with single-issue movements, NGOs and charities. For instance, one MORI survey found that political activism (campaigning for a party) among mature adults has declined marginally in the past thirty years (falling from 18 per cent to 13 per cent), most rapidly between Labour's election in 1997 and its second campaign for office in 2001. In contrast involvement in 'fund raising' and even 'public speaking' for an individual cause increased significantly in the same period, from 22 per cent to 26 per cent and from 11 per cent to 18 per cent respectively. The figures among 16–24-year-olds are more dramatic and speak volumes about the next generation's attitude towards organised politics. The number of young people urging others to vote has fallen from 18 per cent in 1972 to just 6 per cent in 2001. Actual voting has declined alarmingly from 43 to 19 per cent. Meanwhile those involved in 'fund raising' have only slipped from 24 to 21 per cent and the number speaking on behalf of an individual cause has risen from 10 per cent to 13 per cent. Overall, socio-political activism directed at single-issue campaigns has risen, while involvement in party politics has fallen. Worcester and Mortimore's data illustrates that the trends illustrated in this book began long before the Iraq war, the event often erroneously cited as being solely responsible for public disengagement.

This book argues that the underlying cause of this trend is triangulation. Triangulation is the political tactic of shifting party policy in to a broadly perceived centre ground in order to increase electability and outmanoeuvre the opposition, who subsequently become associated with extremism and anachronism. Specifically this book is concerned with the effects of triangulation within the Labour Party between 1994 and 1997, a process that was borrowed directly from America. In the United States it heralded under Bill Clinton's presidency the ending of the Democratic Party's often difficult, but indispensable, relationship with the white working class based upon welfare, protectionism and big government spending. The strategy was pioneered by Bill Morris, a staffer of Clinton's while he was governor of Arkansas who otherwise campaigned solely for Republicans (even Clinton hated him, delivering a savage left hook to his strategist's jaw during his last gubernatorial campaign). He urged his boss to issue a declaration of independence from both the Republican right and his own party's left to nullify accusations made during the early years of his presidency that he might have a legislative agenda. Clinton's strategy of blunting his ideology to appeal to the sceptical middle class heavily influenced British Labour politicians. This book aims not to provide a detailed narrative of Labour's transformation but to study its effects. In short, triangulation has left our mainstream parties fighting over an ill-defined 'centre'. That centre, not being rooted in an ideological discourse, is prone to move rapidly from left to right. It escapes definition. Indeed, because it is fostered by an opportunistic political process, it *defies* definition.

This has led to severe repercussions for British political discourse. This study seeks not to pass judgement upon those who decided to alter, or indeed drop altogether, ideological discourse in this country in the past decade. It simply assesses the impact of Tony Blair's experiment within his own party upon the wider democratic system. To his defenders he has sought (to quote him directly) to prove that 'the task of national renewal . . . can't be done by returning to the past of staying with the failed policies of the present . . . by replacing one dogma with another'. To his detractors this has resulted in profound vacuity. To some, such as the late Robin Cook, it has even resulted in significant policy errors and the erosion of the powers of Parliament, all 'symptomatic of a wider problem from New Labour's lacking of an ideological anchor'.

This study is dedicated to answering three simple questions. The first is what happened in the 2005 general election. It studies the shifts in support among economic groups and from party to party. In so doing it addresses party loyalty, attitudes towards the government and the public's favourability towards the alternatives. It is our contention that the 2005 results were considerably more significant than has been appreciated by most studies and commentators. In particular we argue that the returns provide ample evidence of a de-alignment, mostly slow but sure (although in some areas startlingly dramatic), among the British electorate. To reduce the evidence crudely, public loyalty towards two-party politics is in a process of steady erosion. As recently as 1997 the public gave the lion's share of their votes to either Labour or the Conservatives: Labour received 44 per cent, the Conservatives 31 per cent and the Liberal Democrats 17 per cent. In 2005 the public came remarkably close to creating a three-horse race, Labour receiving 37 per cent, the Tories 33 per cent and the Liberal Democrats 22 per cent. Moreover, the media has rightly challenged the 'mandate' that the Prime Minister claimed he had won in May 2005. He took the lowest share of the electorate that a winning party has ever secured, just 22 per cent.

The second task is to ask why this took place. Whilst this survey accepts traditional arguments about the significance of social mobility, upheaval and change, it suggests that the most important factor has been the triangulation of the Labour Party. Labour's attempts after its defeat in 1992 to move to and dominate the centre ground have had enormous consequences for political debate, activism and management in modern Britain. In essence the motor for political and electoral change has been the parties themselves. Illustrated here are both how they came to be where they are now and the impact that journey has had upon their patterns of demographic support. It is important to stress that this book does not give credence to historical determinism, a fatalistic creed that argues that the position in which we now find ourselves was inevitable. This is an argument readily accepted by many of the major political actors quoted in this book, who prefer to claim that their views and policies are based on the evolution of long-term, deeply held political convictions. Or else, increasingly in the case of New Labour, of grim economic realism. Rather, this book affords an opportunity to 're-historicise' the past and to explain in some detail the central role of accident, chance and personality upon the development of the modern parties. When one accepts the role of historical accident, one accepts the artificial nature of much of the edifice upon which the parties build their manifestos and construct their appeal. A primary aim of this study is nothing less than the Confucian dream of 'correcting the language': to explain for instance what 'liberal democracy' really means and how it came about.

The final question before us is that of what the prospects are for change, or what could happen next. It is obviously valuable to analyse the capacity for the parties to adapt to a world of dealignment and, in particular, to the New Politics. The latter is not an ideological or even theoretical term but merely a convenient 'catch-all phrase' to describe the current political environment. It is an environment created by a number of historical factors and revolutions in communication that do not directly concern this study; indeed, we take its existence as simple fact. But importantly, it is an environment within which party labels lose their significance, locality and constituency politics are paramount, and the public apparently thirsts for personality, honesty, blunt talking and brave policy alternatives. At issue here are the shape of things to come and the ability of parties to survive the process of triangulation and dealignment. As one should be wary of forcing templates upon past behaviour in discussing how parties came to be, so too must one be cautious of making grand predictions when discussing how they might end up. Nonetheless, by studying parties as they currently stand, their strengths, weakness and past actions, it is possible to identify patterns of behaviour and suggest possible future trends. The mainstream parties are currently prisoners of the past, basing future policies upon perceived past successes or philosophical heritage.

Although these three questions are the immediate concerns of this book, its structure is not based entirely around them. Instead each party is taken in turn, using them to illustrate, and to a certain extent narrate, the process and products of triangulation. Chapter 1 deals directly with the first question, by analysing in depth the 2005 returns. Chapter 2 studies the Labour Party and explains the history of triangulation, a political process that mirrors that which took place in the United States and to a certain extent Australasia. The move of the Labour Party from democratic socialism to the politics of the opportunistic centre is the catalyst for the changes studied in the rest of the book. Chapter 3 looks at the impact of Labour's transformation upon the Conservative Party. It argues that the Tories have proved unable to respond effectively to New Labour, have produced an internal response that is both contradictory and capable of erupting into broader ideological conflict. We also argue that a process of internal triangulation became apparent in the recent leadership contest. Chapter 4 deals with the rise of a third party in the wake of triangulation and whether or not the Liberal Democrats can provide a clear alternative to the two-party system. Finally, Chapter 5 looks at the increase in support for independent, fourth-party campaigns. The litmus test of the current political climate has been the capacity of these groups to gain remarkable levels of support from those who feel disenfranchised by the process of triangulation.

In a world that boasts new environmental challenges, a new post-industrial economy and new technological breakthroughs, the mainstream parties have evolved some new policies but no new coherent ideologies. It can be argued that this is the cause of dealignment and disengagement. This is not because we live in a post-ideological age as some party leaderships would have their membership, the press and the public believe. The rise of Islamic fundamentalism in the Middle East, the new left in Germany and neo-conservatism in

America would suggest that such a notion is simply absurd. But in Britain our major parties have not yet adapted to the post-Cold War era by evolving new philosophies in which to ground policy or simply the big ideas necessary to engage the public. It is not necessary to place a value judgement upon this current situation – although throughout the book conclusions are drawn that imply that triangulation has resulted in incoherence, the blurring of party lines, confusion of language and declining activism and engagement. It can even be demonstrated to have led to errors of policy, or at least a blindness to viable alternatives and controversial economic and political strategies that might have some genuine value yet pose too great a risk to a party desperately seeking the centre ground. Examples of these are plentiful in this survey.

Political analysis does not take place in a vacuum and it is impossible to deny that the authors do have a personal interest in the current political situation. First, we are historians. As such we regard it as important that past events are not misappropriated and that ignorance does not shroud any understanding of the journey Britain has taken in the last twenty years. Some politicians claim too readily that their current policies are based upon irreversible historical trends when in fact they are based upon sheer historical accident or clear-cut and often controversial choices. Others seem to ignore that past altogether or even rewrite it to justify policy. Moreover, as historians we see the value in bringing together the best elements of politics, sociology and journalism in our study. The historical discipline is one based on synthesis (what some might call daylight robbery), and in intending this work to be both academic and reportage we hope it is both rigorous and accessible.

Second, we too are a part of history and are both activists. We feel drawn to participate in politics. We have very different perspectives but we both wish to take part in the process that ultimately governs and directs our lives. Politics is simply the operation of society, the means by which people organise themselves. To withdraw from it is to withdraw from community itself. This book represents a personal response to the changes in politics of the last decade. Our generation put down its roots at the end of the Cold War, an era marked by an uneasy transition from one politics to another. It is a generation both steeped in the language of fixed ideology and uncomfortably aware of its anachronism. This study is partially an attempt to understand the current confusion of sensibilities in order that we might conceive of a new order to replace them.

We have spent a year studying how people vote, why parties no longer command the old loyalties upon which they once depended and what the future is likely to hold, how far parties are capable of adapting to the new order. We hope that both public and politician will read it, for rarely do they share tastes in literature, and that from it we might begin to debate what alternatives there are to our current democratic malaise. Although such statements can often sound puerile, we do aim to speak for (at least an element of) a generation that feels that politics was something their grandparents did. Apathy among the young is of particular concern to our society because they nominally form the governments of the future. Young people enter politics to change the world. But no one, least of all the Labour Party, seems currently interested in this noble, almost existential, yearning for radical change. The reason for this, its impact and the prospects for change are the key to this book.

1

The changing electoral landscape

In his address 'A warning against the force of habit' Günter Grass made the simple but powerful point that nothing in history is constant. Even the most familiar aspects of our lives, even those things to which we are most habituated and scarcely even notice, are susceptible to sudden change. To no area of human life is this more applicable than to politics. Elsewhere in his writings, particularly in the essay 'What Shall We Tell Our Children?' and his book *The Tin Drum*, Grass intimates that while no conscious responsibility for political changes can be identified, unconscious complicity can be attributed to all who are members of a polity. The change that is an inescapable if unwelcome feature of political life occurs gradually, even imperceptibly, through the silent and unknowing conspiracy of the unconcerned masses.

Although Grass has devoted his career to exploring the role played by ordinary Germans in the rise of Nazism, his historical assumptions about political change could readily be applied to any number of other examples. Contemporary Britain is no exception: although we have become habituated to a particular set of political patterns, some of the most familiar features of British political life have recently been subject to remarkable change at the unconscious instigation of the electorate. These in turn have altered the ground on which the edifices of political parties are built and have presented political leaders with new problems and challenges for the future. This chapter charts the most significant electoral shifts and introduces some of the key issues facing British politicians as a result.

Milburn's mea culpa and the collapse of Labour's constituency

Seven weeks after their third consecutive election victory, Labour's campaign co-ordinator, Alan Milburn, warned the party against complacency in an article in the *Times*. Although he shied away from using the word 'Pyrrhic' to describe his party's victory, he nevertheless suggested that its success could contain the seeds of future defeat. Despite having been returned with another sizeable majority, Labour had suffered a massive decline in popular support. Parliamentary seats had been lost in their dozens and majorities cut to such an extent that at the next general election a bare minimum of twenty seats would be in serious jeopardy. Among the young, among the aspirant and skilled working class, in the East of England and in Greater London, Labour support had 'slumped' to the point where 'an historic fourth term' in office seemed uncertain at best. Dissatisfaction, Milburn hinted, was strong and would grow to engulf New Labour unless something was done to recoup millions of lost votes.

A cynical reader might have dismissed Milburn's article as insincere, as a theatrical display of self-flagellation designed to counter post-election accusations of arrogance. But even a cynic could not accuse Milburn of being wrong. His central claim, that Labour's electoral strength had been severely weakened, was absolutely correct. Its majority had been cut from 160 to sixty-six, a fall far greater than Margaret Thatcher's Conservative government had experienced between its second and third election victories, and greater even than that experienced between the victories of 1987 and 1992. The forty-seven seats that Labour had lost were distributed around the country, from Dumfriesshire, Clydesdale & Tweeddale to Torridge & West Devon – suggesting a nationwide swing away from the party – but were most heavily concentrated in Greater London, where it lost eleven seats, and the Eastern region, where it lost seven. In London Labour's share of the vote dropped by an average of 8.4 per cent relative to 2001, well in excess of the national average of 6 per cent. In some metropolitan constituencies up to 21 per cent of the vote was lost (Poplar & Canning Town) and formerly 'safe' seats became frighteningly marginal. Similarly MORI's final aggregate analysis of the polls confirms that since 2001 Labour's support has declined by 13 per cent among voters aged between twenty-five and thirty-four and by 9 per cent amongst C2 voters.

If Milburn was correct, however, he was telling only part of the story. Writing as Labour's election campaign co-ordinator in a daily newspaper, he was concerned primarily with the immediate damage done to his party's parliamentary majority and the proximate challenges it would face. Longer-term trends and gradual shifts in the topography of the political landscape did not fall within his ken. Yet, while the loss of votes and seats is worthy of attention, a more significant alteration has occurred which suggests not merely that Labour's future as a government had been threatened but also that the social constituency upon which it has traditionally relied had collapsed.

At elections the Labour Party's fortunes have historically depended on particular sections of society and specific areas of the country more than others. This is partly a reflection of the ideological focus and origins of the party and partly a result of traditional political sympathies amongst the electorate. From its inception the Labour Party was concerned above all else with the condition of the working classes and of the poorer elements of British society. In elections it deliberately targeted these groups and succeeded in those constituencies which had a high density of working-class voters and a noticeable dependence on industrial employment. Although it later gained some measure of support amongst skilled workers and the middle classes, the party tended to perform best in the industrial north of Britain, in Greater London, amongst semi- and unskilled workers and amongst the unemployed. By the second half of the twentieth century Labour could depend on the return of at least 200 MPs at a general election, still overwhelmingly concentrated in the North, the North-West, Yorkshire and Humberside and in the capital (see Table 1.1). Even in the party's darkest days, when it was in opposition and suffering from crippling losses, MPs were returned for some constituencies in these regions with over 65 per cent of the vote. In 1983, for example, when the party held 209 seats nationally (its worst performance since 1935), it still commanded a 45.2 per cent majority in Liverpool Riverside, a heavily industrialised constituency with a high rate of unemployment and deprivation.[1]

Table 1.1: Seats held by Labour in selected regions of England, 1974–2005

	Feb. 1974	Oct. 1974	1979	1983	1987	1992	1997	2001	2005
North	28	29	29	26	27	29	32	32	32
North West	48	51	45	35	36	44	60	60	57
Yorkshire and the Humber	38	38	34	28	33	34	47	47	44
London	50	51	42	26	23	35	57	55	44
Total seats held in above regions	164	169	150	115	119	142	196	194	177
Total of all seats held by Labour	301	319	269	209	229	271	418	413	356
% of MPs from above regions	54.5	53.0	55.8	55.0	52.0	52.4	46.9	47.0	49.7

Data from David Butler and Dennis Kavanagh, *British General Election series*.

In his article Milburn rightly drew attention to the swing away from the Labour Party in the skilled working class at the 2005 election. Along with semi- and unskilled workers (group DE), this group has buttressed the Labour Party since its election to government in 1997. At that election 50 per cent of C2 voters and 59 per cent of DE voters supported the party and there is little doubt that they were instrumental in helping to deliver the massive landslide that swept John Major's Conservative Party from office. Four years later, at the 2001 election, there was a slight decline in their support, C2 votes dipping to 49 per cent and DE to 55 per cent. By 2005, however, Labour's approval in these socio-economic groups dropped sharply to 40 per cent and 48 per cent respectively. Constituencies with high concentrations of skilled, semi-skilled and unskilled workers, such as Gravesham in Kent, were suddenly and unexpectedly lost. This diminution of support is surprising enough in the short term but is all the more shocking given that the level of approbation which Labour received from skilled workers was the lowest since 1992 (and only 4 per cent better than in 1987) and that from semi- and unskilled workers the lowest since 1987. Tellingly, the gap between Labour and other parties in these groups has also declined. In 1997, for example, Labour enjoyed a 38 point lead over the

Conservatives and a 46 point lead over the Liberal Democrats amongst DE voters. In 2005 its lead had been reduced to 23 percentage points over the Conservatives and 30 points over the Liberal Democrats. Although Labour's dominance as the party of preference for these socio-economic sections of society is not in any doubt, it is striking that the foundation for its support has decreased. More significantly, the manner in which the drift away from Labour in groups C2 and DE has been distributed around Britain suggests an even more fundamental shift in the structure of electoral politics.

Although it is difficult to translate these trends into a detailed electoral picture – there being limited socio-economic data available at a local level – they are nevertheless reflected in Labour's performance in those seats which it retained. In some industrial constituencies, where the proportion of skilled and unskilled workers is known to be high, comparatively sound majorities were replaced by marginal victories. In Edinburgh South Labour took only 33.2 per cent of the vote at the 2005 general election, compared with 42.2 per cent in 2001 (a drop of 21.3 per cent) and its majority fell from 14.8 per cent to 0.95 per cent. Similarly in Loughborough Labour's share of the vote was 16.7 per cent lower than in 2001 and its majority went down from 14.4 per cent in 2001 to 4.3 per cent in 2005. This picture is repeated even more forcefully in seats which have previously been considered very 'safe' for Labour. In Sheffield Central (which has been represented by Richard Caborn since 1983) Labour enjoyed over 60 per cent of the vote in each election from 1983 to 2001, yet in 2005 its share declined to 49.9 per cent.[2] Likewise in Burnley Labour recorded its lowest share of the vote in twenty-two years, 38.5 per cent.[3] Indeed, in those regions which have the highest proportion of C2 and DE voters and which have historically also been the heartland of the Parliamentary Labour Party, there has been a steady and marked decline in support for the party. In Yorkshire and Humberside, the North and the North-West the swing may not have significantly affected the return of Labour MPs to Westminster but majorities have been seriously diminished and the party's share of the vote dramatically reduced. The majority of constituencies in these regions show a decline in Labour's share of the vote well above the national average and a significant number returned an MP with a share of the vote that was up to 15 percentage points lower than in 2001. Whether former Labour voters are simply declining to vote or are actively voting against the party is immaterial: the impression remains that more people who used to vote Labour are no longer doing so.

Similarly, in those regions which Milburn mentioned as being of particular concern – the East of England and Greater London – it is noticeable that Labour's performance was poorest in those constituencies whose electorate is known to be dominated by C2 and DE voters. In Poplar & Canning Town, covering the Isle of Dogs in the east of London, where unemployment stood at 8.5 per cent in May 2005[4] and which was part of the fourth most deprived local authority area in Britain,[5] Labour's share of the vote declined by 21.1 percentage points. Just slightly further north, in West Ham, part of the eleventh most deprived area in the country, where 7.8 per cent of the electorate were unemployed, its share of the vote declined by 18.7 points.

The impression that Labour is losing support amongst those sections of society which, when highly concentrated, have provided the foundation of its political strength is repeated when other socio-economic indicators are examined. If no accurate data is available for the socio-economic makeup of different constituencies, there is considerable information available about levels of unemployment. Unemployment is not an ideal indicator of the socio-economic status of constituencies but it can be regarded as an effective reflection of their general standards of living. Moreover, since unemployment is most likely to affect those from lower socio-economic classes, it can be used as an indirect, albeit imperfect, indicator of the proportion of C2 and DE voters in a particular area.

Examining the unemployment figures for May 2005 in relation to the election results presents an interesting picture. At the time of the election the national average level of unemployment (not seasonally adjusted) was given as 3.1 per cent. This level of unemployment or more was experienced in 208 constituencies in England, accounting for slightly less than a third of all constituencies in the United Kingdom. Of these, 197 were held by Labour at the 2001 election, including all of the 100 English constituencies with the highest levels of unemployment. At the 2005 election Labour lost sixteen of these seats and overall experienced an above-average reduction in its share of the vote of 8 percentage points. In the 100 constituencies with the highest unemployment in England, this swing increased on average to 9 points and among the top 25 to 11 points. It is more striking that if one examines all of the 208 English constituencies with unemployment at or above the national average, a clear relationship can be observed between the level of unemployment and the decline in Labour's share of the vote. At a 5 per cent level of significance, there is more than enough evidence to support the derivation of a relationship which posits that the higher the level of unemployment in a constituency, the greater the swing away from Labour. Although this cannot necessarily be used to suggest a causal relationship between unemployment and a swing away from Labour, it does at least illustrate the regularity of the decline in support for the party amongst the poorest members of society.[6] By contrast it can be perceived that Labour has held its support relatively well since 1997 and even increased it since 1983 amongst the wealthier members of society. Amongst women in the highest socio-economic class (14 per cent of voters in 2005), Labour has managed to strengthen its support since 2001 and its support base in this group has declined by only 1 percentage point since 1997.

While the most obvious effect of this shift in voting patterns was Labour's loss of several seats in London and in the East of England region at the 2005 election, it is of greater historical significance that support for the party amongst its traditional social constituency has been declining. Although Labour remained the party of preference amongst skilled, semi-skilled and unskilled labouring voters, amongst the unemployed and in the northern regions, its lead over opposition parties is diminishing and it no longer commands either an absolute majority amongst these voting groups or the automatic backing of its former social constituents. Those whom the Labour Party was originally designed to represent and who previously gave it unerring support have turned away in an unprecedented fashion. This should not be under-estimated in scale, scope or importance. Even bearing in mind the redrafting of Clause 4 in 1995, it is still surprising that the party, which maintains close links with the trade unions and continues to receive significant financial contributions from labour associations, should be losing votes amongst the urban working classes. Indeed, in a MORI poll conducted in September 2004, which surveyed people who viewed parties' policy towards trade unions as an important factor in determining how they would vote in 2005, fewer declared that they believed the Labour Party to be best placed to serve their interests than the other major parties. In this poll 33 per cent said that they did not know which party had the best policy on trade unions, 25 per cent believed the Liberal Democrats would represent them best, 23 per cent indicated they would vote Conservative on this basis and a mere 19 per cent said they were likely to support the Labour Party. This is the first time since accurate polling in this field began that Labour has not commanded a significant lead amongst those who believed policy towards trade unions to be a key election issue. To put this in a slightly different way in a wider context, this is the first time that the party of labour has been unable to command the 'natural' support of those members of the labour force whose conditions it still remains committed to improving.

This raises the question of why Labour's historical social constituency has been collapsing. The simple but not insubstantial answer is that fewer C2 and DE voters and fewer people in the north of England and Greater London feel a strong affinity with the Labour Party. Although it continues to enjoy strong approval among those social groups and in those regions which have previously provided the most reliable support, the tie which binds many to the party is becoming weaker. The crucial harness – dictated by any number of concerns but historically connected (causally or otherwise) with social and economic conditions – which willingly yoked certain segments of the electorate to the Labour Party is being shaken off to a greater extent. More and more Labour voters from its 'core' areas of support are turning to other parties.

This phenomenon is not necessarily a result of voters feeling any less 'Labour' in their outlook. In reality it is the case that skilled, semi-skilled and unskilled workers in the north of England and in Greater London feel as attached as ever to 'Labour' ideas. Although there has been very little difference between Labour and Conservative policy on social issues in recent years, voters continue to stress their preference for the Labour Party over any other. Whether or not they are aware of the details of policy or not (and the evidence seems to suggest that they are not), many voters in Labour 'heartlands' appear to have a deep-rooted faith in the Labour Party's capacity to provide better government with respect to welfare and other social issues. It is, moreover, social issues, such as healthcare and education, which are regularly revealed as the most important stated determinants of voting behaviour.

Despite the persistence of Labour's success in key policy areas, however, it is clear that people are becoming more disenchanted with New Labour as a political party. Although they may like what 'Labour' stands for, supporters from its heartlands no longer associate those values so strongly with Tony Blair's New Labour. A breach has emerged between the wider Labour movement and its electoral participants on the one hand and the Labour Party itself on the other. This could perhaps be seen as a consequence of the actions of the Labour leadership itself. In many ways the collapse of Labour's traditional electoral base can be seen as the party becoming a victim of its own success. It is the result of a conscious political effort made since 1997 to rid the party of its more traditional associations. So effective was this that by 1999 John Monks, then general secretary of the TUC, said that he felt those who had voted Labour before the 1990s were 'being accused of poor judgement' and 'seen as embarrassingly elderly relatives'. 'Old' Labour was consciously shelved in favour of a more 'modern' version of the party which bore more similarity to the approach of Margaret Thatcher than to that of Michael Foot. Despite some token attempts to pacify the stalwarts of 'Old' Labour, as time went on fewer traditional Labour voters had confidence in the leadership's adherence to 'Labour' values. Blair's New Labour was perceived as being more occupied with the careful management of the media and the tactical determination of policy than with the pursuit of Labour's historical socialist democratic goals. Ideology was seen as having been replaced with 'spin'. Trust in the party, amongst supporters and in the country at large, plummeted. In the run-up to the 2005 election this decline of trust was accelerated by a number of issues but there was none as significant as the handling of the war in Iraq. The details of the political wranglings which surrounded the beginning of the conflict were to a large number of people something of a mystery, but it was nevertheless felt by many that Britain had entered a war having been deceived by its Prime Minister.

Although the Hutton inquiry into the death of Dr David Kelly failed to point the finger of guilt at any senior government figure and declined to comment on the validity of the case for war, media coverage conveyed the impression that Blair and his Cabinet could not be trusted. The leadership had first led the party away from Labour's core values, away from its emphasis on corporatism and social justice, and had then led the country into an unnecessary war on the basis of misinformation. The Prime Minister had deceived his own party and deceived the country as a whole. Hence, while voters could say without much difficulty that the Labour Party had the best policies on the most important issues in domestic politics, some could no longer bring themselves to support the party they had backed so loyally for so many years.

The Liberal Democrats, electoral volatility and localism

Given that since 2001 the Liberal Democrats have increased their share of the vote by an average of 4 percentage points (a 21.1 per cent rise) while the Conservatives have registered no change, some commentators have suggested that the decline in Labour's support puts the former in an ideal position to make massive gains in future. It is true that the Liberal Democrats gained substantially – even remarkably – from the Labour Party. At a national level 15 per cent of the 28 per cent of those who turned away from Labour voted Liberal Democrat, compared to 8 per cent who voted Conservative. At a constituency level the picture was even more impressive. On the one hand, sixteen seats were taken, thirteen of them from Labour, and recorded some spectacular victories, most notably in Brent East, Manchester Withington and Cambridge. On the other hand, even without taking other constituency seats, the increase in the Liberal Democrats' share of the vote was staggering. In Blackburn, held by the Foreign Secretary, Jack Straw, Labour received 22.4 per cent less of the popular vote (a drop of 12.1 percentage points), while the Liberal Democrat candidate increased his share by 79 per cent (6.4 points) relative to 2001, despite remaining in third place. In Leicester South Labour's share of the vote declined from 54.5 per cent in 2001 to 39.3 per cent in 2005, while the Liberal Democrats increased their share by 13.4 points (77.9 per cent), solidifying their position as the second party of preference. Elsewhere in the country the pattern was repeated. In Brentford & Isleworth the Liberal Democrats took 68.9 per cent more votes and increased their share by 9.3 points, while in third place, at the same time as support for the Labour Party declined by 23.9 per cent (12.5 points). The examples are numerous and at a first glance appear to have occurred regardless of the tactical situation.

It is, however, too easy to present the Liberal Democrats as the 'next big thing' on the basis of a 4 point increase in their national share of the vote. If the distribution of their vote is analysed, it appears that this seemingly impressive gain should be viewed not so much with optimism as with scepticism and concern.

Before the 2005 election the Liberal Democrats expected to perform particularly well in the south of England. In 2001 over a third of their sixty-two MPs came from the South-East and South-West and there were a large number of seats in which their candidate had come a close second. There was every indication that they were poised to do well in this part of the country and no fewer than twenty-seven of their top fifty target seats were in the South-East and South-West of England. Most of them were held by the Conservatives in 2001.

On the night of 5 May, however, senior Liberal Democrats were astonished when the exit polls started to emerge. Rather than the sizeable advances their election co-ordinator, Lord Razzall, had expected, their performance in the south of England appeared stunted. Although Razzall was right in predicting that they would increase their share of the vote in the South-East, the South-West, the West Midlands and the East Midlands, the progress they made was restrained, to say the least. In the South-West they gained only an extra 1.4 per cent of the vote, while in the South-East they gained an additional 1.7 per cent but actually lost two seats. In many of the constituencies which they had seen as being 'ripe for the picking', such as Isle of Wight (eighth on their list of target seats), they lost a significant proportion of the vote.

It was, in fact, only in the Labour heartlands that the Liberal Democrats augmented their share of the vote appreciably and it was their performance in these regions which skewed the national picture in such a way as to produce the impressive gain of 4 percentage points.

In the regions in the north of England they gained more than twice as many votes as in the southern areas, and in the North-East they gained an additional 6.6 per cent of the vote relative to 2001. What is most striking about this is that, although there is no absolutely robust pattern to discern, Liberal Democrat candidates recorded their most impressive successes in constituencies which continued to return Labour MPs with solid if much reduced majorities. 'Safe' Labour seats tended to provide the Liberal Democrats with the greatest increases in their share of the vote. In the more deprived London constituencies, where the depreciation in Labour support was most pronounced, the Liberal Democrats benefited greatly. In Brent South, which in May 2005 had an unemployment rate of 8.1 per cent, they increased their share of the vote by 91.7 per cent (9.9 percentage points), while Labour took 19.8 per cent of the vote (14.5 points) less than in 2001. In Vauxhall, part of the twenty-third most deprived local authority in the country with an unemployment rate of 7.3 per cent, they gained 97 per cent of the votes lost by the Labour candidate and increased their share of the vote by 29.9 per cent (6 points). Even more pronounced results were evident in the north of England. Bradford North, part of the thirtieth most deprived local authority in Britain, was the site of a massive swing of 12.5 points to the Liberal Democrats from Labour and the Conservatives and the pattern was repeated in constituencies such as Leeds West.

This pattern is positive in that it does present the Liberal Democrats as the heirs to the fragmented remains of Labour's social constituency. The regions and constituencies in which the minority party performed more admirably in terms of an increased share of the vote were precisely those with high concentrations of C2 and DE voters in which Labour had suffered the greatest damage to its historical base of support. Since newspaper polls throughout the campaign consistently demonstrated that the Liberal Democrats were perceived as more left wing than Labour, it is extremely tempting, if rather dangerous, to suggest that the Liberal Democrats are assuming the electoral mantle of the Labour movement cast off by Tony Blair's New Labour.

There is, however, a much more negative slant to put on the pattern of Liberal Democrat gains. At a national level their apparent promise can be seen as misleading on account of highly localised advances. Although they increased their national share of the vote by 4 percentage points, it seems that their success in this respect was primarily due to the fact that they can be presented as Labour's primary heirs in its former heartlands. The relatively uninspiring increase in their share of the vote in the south of England was counterbalanced by a strong showing in the industrial and urban northern regions. This makes the national parliamentary picture less impressive. While it is significant that the Liberal Democrats have gained votes most particularly from Labour in its strongest areas, this must be viewed against the position in which this places them for the future. Gains in the popular vote of between 7 and 21 points in the North-East, the North-West and the West Midlands make them appear to be a more credible political force in certain constituencies but do not mean that they will be likely to increase their parliamentary strength in these areas at coming elections. The general impression to be gained from these regions is that where the Liberal Democrats succeeded in increasing their share of the vote substantially, they were nevertheless still left a very long way from being able to challenge Labour incumbents. In Manchester Central, for example, the Liberal Democrat candidate gained an impressive 9.0 percentage points relative to the 2001 election, an increase of 57.3 per cent. The Labour candidate, however, was still returned with a majority of 33.4 per cent, leaving the Liberal Democrat trailing far behind in second place. Again, in Birmingham Hall Green, the Liberals increased their share of the vote by 119.2 per cent (10.5 percentage points) but were left in third place behind a Conservative candidate and a Labour MP who was returned with a 16.5 per cent majority. This pattern was repeated once more in Wythenshawe & Sale East, where the Liberal Democrats gained an extra 74 per cent of the vote (a gain of 9.1 percentage points) but were again left trailing in third place while the Labour candidate was returned with a 29.9 per cent majority.

These are perhaps some of the most extreme examples, but they are not uncharacteristic of the general pattern which is observable in the Liberal Democrats' performance. Considering that their national success owes more to their acquisition of Labour's fragmenting social constituency in urban and industrial areas, it seems that they are in fact approaching a parliamentary glass ceiling. Their share of the vote has increased, but at the same time it has increased most significantly in areas in which it would be necessary in future to increase their share by at least 20 percentage points in order to take certain constituency seats.

At a more localised level the picture becomes even less inspiring for the Liberal Democrats. If they increased their share of the vote in Labour's traditional heartlands, they did not necessarily do so because they were perceived as a better choice for government. While the personalities of the party are generally seen as being trustworthy and likeable, the Liberal Democrats' policies not only fail to attract significant support but are virtually unknown. With respect to the most important issues facing Britain, such as healthcare and education, they are believed to be less preferable than those of both of the other major parties and other alternatives. Taken as a whole, their policies are not seen as embodying the best programme of action for Britain. The Liberal Democrats' success in Labour heartlands is therefore not a consequence of their own merits but a result of their rivals' failures. As New Labour has achieved ascendancy in British politics, it has alienated a considerable number of its former supporters. Unable to bring themselves to vote for the Conservatives, those who wished to continue voting (and a noticeable proportion did not) switched their support to the Liberal Democrats. In contrast to the Conservatives, they were an appealing alternative. It was not that traditional Labour voters actually saw much that was desirable in Liberal Democrat policies, but rather that they saw the Liberal Democrats as a convenient opportunity to register their dissatisfaction without troubling their conscience too greatly. As a party of the left, the Liberal Democrats were sufficiently close to 'Old' Labour not to be unattractive but distant enough from New Labour for a vote to be significant.

The appearance of the Liberal Democrats as the party of protest in Labour's former heartlands may therefore have boosted their national share of the vote, but in an artificial manner. The flow of votes was not 'positive' but 'negative'. In the more depressed areas of the north of England a vote for the Liberal Democrats was most usually a vote against New Labour rather than a sign of approbation for Charles Kennedy and his party's policies. There was no strong foundation laid on which to build a reliable structure of electoral support for the future; what persuaded people to vote Liberal Democrat in 2005 may not apply at any point in the future. No ties were applied to bind former Labour voters to another party. The support which the Liberal Democrats gained – or appeared to gain – in 2005 may not recur.

What is more, even if the Liberal Democrats manage to retain the level of their support amongst Labour's former electoral base, there is no 'positive' indication that they will be able to increase their share of the vote beyond this point. Given that swings of up to 20 percentage points will be necessary at a future election for Liberal Democrat candidates to unseat Labour incumbents, the lack of tangible reasons for people to vote *for* the Liberal Democrats will prove to be an almost insurmountable obstacle to success. While the anti-Labour vote is growing in its historical heartlands, it is not growing in such a fashion that suggests that voters would be prepared to go much beyond mere protest. Indeed, the appearance of the protest vote phenomenon may have been to the Liberal Democrats' benefit in 2005, but it cannot help but retain an uncertain and unreliable form as a basis for electoral success in future. The glass ceiling which the party seems to have reached in many northern seats may in fact turn out to be more of a concrete barrier. At both a national and a more localised level therefore the collapse of Labour's traditional electoral base does not mean that the future is quite so rosy for the parliamentary Liberal Democrats.

If, however, the Liberal Democrats did benefit from the dis-integration of Labour's traditional base of support without necessarily making many corresponding parliamentary gains, this implies that there has been a noticeable shift in voting preferences which are not necessarily linked to policy preferences in themselves. The simple observation that more people from Labour's traditional social constituency abandoned the party of labour is worth revisiting in this respect. If a greater proportion of the people who in previous years comprised a dependable voting block are no longer so clearly attached to a particular party, it is only sensible to posit that more people are presently willing to change their vote. While it is true that in many cases at the 2005 election, the Liberal Democrats benefited from this willingness to change allegiance, this can also be seen as an indication that the electorate is becoming more volatile or, to put it another way, that voting patterns are becoming more fluid.

In support of this conjecture, a MORI/*Financial Times* poll conducted at the start of the 2005 election campaign showed that 41 per cent of people were prepared to change their mind about who to vote for. Although there is nothing odd about voters being willing to alter their opinions, the study demonstrated that the proportion of the electorate who were considering changing their vote was higher than at any election for eighteen years. At the elections between 1987 and 2001 an average of 29 per cent of people said there was a chance they might change their mind before voting. This suggests that as Labour's social constituency has collapsed, a great and growing body of people has emerged who do not consider themselves attached to any one party.

In the same vein MORI's final aggregate analysis of the 2005 election indicated that a striking number of voters had changed their vote since 2001. Twenty-eight per cent of those who voted Labour at the 2001 election, 22 per cent of those who voted Liberal Democrat and 10 per cent of those who voted Conservative were reported as having changed their vote at the 2005 election. What is more interesting, and more telling about this poll, however, is the manner in which people changed their vote. While 15 per cent of those who voted Labour at the 2001 election changed their minds to vote Liberal Democrat in 2005, 8 per cent voted Conservative. Importantly, of those who turned away from the Liberal Democrats, twice as many voted Conservative (12 per cent) as voted for Labour (6 per cent) and of those who supported the Conservatives in 2001, three times as many switched to the Liberal Democrats (6 per cent) as changed to vote Labour (2 per cent). None of these changes, it should be noted, were matched by any significant changes in patterns of support for the different parties with respect to specific policy areas. These shifts in actual voting patterns not only reinforce the impression of a dissipation of Labour's backing, but also suggest a varying attitude towards opposition to the party of government, which in turn indicates a noticeable fluidity in voting preferences.

This fluidity is perhaps best expressed as a perceived collapse in the validity of traditional political distinctions. Parties are increasingly seen as being all too similar and the political centre ground as becoming crowded. This is readily apparent in the manner in which voters around Britain changed their votes in 2005. The fact that most electors who shifted their support from the Liberal Democrats moved to the Conservatives and vice versa could indicate that some people saw the party to which they transferred their allegiance as the better placed to provide opposition. Given that studies reproduced in newspapers during the election campaign repeatedly showed the public to perceive the Liberal Democrats as being left wing, the Labour Party as being centrist and the Conservative Party as being right wing, it is interesting in itself that voters should have been willing to move from one end of the political spectrum to the other. This might be taken by some as evidence of tactical voting: voters shifted their allegiance because they believed it would be a better means of ousting a Labour candidate in their constituency. The data available, however, confounds this inter-pretation. If former Conservative voters believed that their opposition to the Labour government (represented locally by an incumbent) would be better served by transferring their vote to the Liberal Democrats, it could be anticipated that in Labour–Liberal Democrat marginals there would have been a shift from the Conservatives to the Liberal Democrats and in Labour–Conservative marginals from the Liberal Democrats to the Conservatives. In reality, however, the transfer of votes along the Conservative–Liberal Democrat axis actually conspired to preserve a Labour incumbency. In Hove, for example, the Labour candidate's share of the vote declined by 18.3 per cent (8.4 points) relative to 2001, putting the Conservatives in a position to take the seat. The Conservatives, however, lost 4.7 per cent of the vote (a drop of 1.9 points), a proportion of which went to the Liberal Democrats, thereby allowing a Labour MP to be returned to Westminster with a majority of 0.9 per cent (2001 majority 7.6 per cent). Meanwhile, in Thanet South a 5.6 per cent (2.3 point) drop in the Conservatives' share of the vote, along with a 40.4 per cent (3.8 point) increase in the Liberal Democrats' share cleared the way for a Labour candidate whose share of the vote had declined by 11.6 per cent (5.3 percentage points) to be returned with a 1.6 per cent majority (2001 majority 4.5 per cent). These two examples clearly illustrate that the transfer of votes between opposition parties was not motivated by tactical considerations. As a corollary of this, there are almost too many examples to cite in which votes lost by the Labour Party were distributed evenly between the opposition parties and thereby removed the possibility of a Labour incumbent being toppled. Medway, Edinburgh South, Selby, Gillingham, Dartford, Stroud, High Peak, Stourbridge, Warwick & Leamington, Battersea and Crawley are just a few of the many constituencies in which a non-tactical division of the vote in a clear two-way marginal situation preserved a Labour incumbency (see Table 1.2). Despite the fact that opposition to the Labour Party increased in all of these constituencies, there was no noticeable co-ordination among voters and electoral decisions clearly seem to have been made at a specific or personal level according to fluidly moving attitudes. Conclusively, when national results are analysed, there is no statistical evidence for a correlation between the 2001 majority and the swing to or from particular parties. In aggregate, changes in voting between the 2001 and 2005 elections were categorically not made on tactical grounds and, indeed, the only thing that can be said about the pattern of changes in voting is that there is no reliable pattern.

Table 1.2: The division of votes in selected marginal seats

Constituency	2001 majority	Lab	Con	L D	2005 majority
Dartford	7.4%	42.6% (–5.4%)	41.1% (+0.5%)	10.8% (+2.3%)	1.5%
High Peak	9.3%	39.6% (–7.0%)	38.2% (+0.9%)	20.0% (+3.9%)	1.5%
Edinburgh South	14.0%	33.2% (–6.1%)	24.1% (+1.4%)	32.3% (+7.0%)	0.9%
Selby	4.3%	43.1% (–2.0%)	42.2% (+1.4%)	14.8% (+3.7%)	0.9%
Gillingham	5.4%	41.2% (–3.3%)	40.7% (+1.6%)	14.9% (+1.3%)	0.6%
Stroud	9.1%	39.6% (–7.0%)	39.0% (+1.6%)	14.1% (+3.2%)	0.6%
Medway	9.8%	42.2% (–6.8%)	41.7% (+2.5%)	12.5% (+3.2%)	0.5%
Warwick & Leamington	11.1%	40.6% (–8.2%)	40.1% (+2.5%)	14.8% (+3.7%)	0.5%
Battersea	13.7%	40.4% (–9.9%)	40.0% (+3.5%)	14.6% (+2.5%)	0.4%
Crawley	17.1%	39.2% (–10.2%)	39.0% (+6.8%)	15.5% (+2.8%)	0.1%

The national corollary of the collapse of Labour's social constituency has therefore been not the emergence of the Liberal Democrats as a 'government in waiting' but the development of an increasingly volatile electorate. Unfettered by long-standing political allegiances and unconstrained by traditional conceptions of the political spectrum, British voters are more prepared to be swayed in their intentions than at any other time in political history. Given that on issues of national importance – such as health and education – polls have shown little change in recent years, as electoral volatility has increased, more locally relevant matters must have acquired a much greater significance in voters' eyes.

Candidates do not seem to have been entirely unaware of this fact and campaigns have been growing increasingly tailored to meet these specific and sensitive concerns. Since 1992 those with pretensions to Westminster have been recorded more and more frequently as saying that their campaigns were conducted with remarkable independence from the party centre.[7] By 2001 a local focus had become a favourite for those campaigning without the benefit of an established name and by 2005 localism had acquired an essential role for the overwhelming majority of candidates. Far from being reduced merely to parroting their party's manifesto pledges, candidates on the stump were observed leaving their party's national proposals behind. This is not to say that any candidate forsook their party allegiances, but rather that they were conscious of a more flexible electorate who were likely to be swayed by concentration on issues of immediate and specific appeal. Election materials published throughout the country demonstrate candidates paying more attention to extremely local concerns – such as the closing of a much-loved pub or worries over vagrancy and begging – than to matters of national concern. In flyers distributed to constituents, candidates repeatedly stressed their commitment to local causes and their local links – this despite the fact that many of the matters discussed in election materials were strictly the preserve of local councils rather than of members of Parliament. One Conservative example is particularly revealing of this trend. Jeremy Hunt (Conservative, South West Surrey) structured his successful election campaign around four separate 'local' campaigns, dealing with such matters as the graffiti around Farnham station and the preservation of a second fire engine for Haslemere fire station. His election addresses made almost no mention of the economy, national healthcare, education or foreign affairs. For Hunt and for the overwhelming majority of candidates, localism was seen as the key to gaining votes in individual constituencies. Crucially, this narrow focus would have been neither possible nor necessary had it not been for the increased volatility of the British electorate. The ascendancy of localism is the expression and consequence of the disintegration of traditional voting patterns and the emergence of a fluid, variable and almost unpredictable electorate.

Looking to the future: problems

Confronted with a volatile electorate that is confounding both traditional assumptions and contemporary expectations, political parties are obliged to tackle a series of new challenges. While these challenges ultimately derive from electoral changes, they engage with longer-running party political issues and inevitably pose demanding questions of direction, policy and appeal.

Labour
No Labour analyst or politician denies that voters are abandoning their party. Contrary to the impression given by senior party officials, however, this swing is occurring most markedly in those areas and in those social groups who have historically provided Labour with its staunchest backing. Whether people are simply declining to vote for the party they formerly supported or are consciously moving into opposition, New Labour is experiencing the first obvious signs of a collapse in its electoral base. This begs the obvious question of what is to be done?

The problem, however, is not as simple as it at first appears. Despite the fact that he does not seem to have appreciated – or accepted – the sheer extent of the diminution in Labour support, Alan Milburn's advocacy of continuing reform is typical of the instant reaction of most party analysts. Yet although reform is an attractive political word that comes readily to mind, it may not necessarily be so easy to give it a concrete form or to translate it into reality. Internal party political issues and potential electoral reactions appear to be major obstacles in the way of any reaction to the collapse of Labour's social constituency.

The New Labour 'project', which from 1994 turned Labour from a democratic socialist party into a centrist party with a soft-left leaning, may have been a popular political transformation, but it has by no means received the unanimous approbation of MPs. Indeed, as New Labour has developed and attempted to continue its innovatory and centrist progress, the parliamentary party has become increasingly fractured and disunited. In some of the areas which are regarded as of crucial importance to the identity of Tony Blair's New Labour, the leadership has experienced some of the worst rebellions since the Corn Laws. In a study on dissent within the Parliamentary Labour Party, Philip Cowley and Mark Stuart have demonstrated that in the period 2001–2005, there were large and threatening revolts over flagship policies in education, criminal justice, immigration, health and social services, industrial relations and foreign affairs.[8] In other words, as New Labour has endeavoured to continue its 'reforming' crusade, it has met increasing opposition from members of its own parliamentary party. In light of this it is questionable whether further reform in the same vein is politically possible. If, however, MPs are unlikely to want a 'Newer' Labour Party, as Milburn seems to suggest, then they must ask themselves what sort of a party they want it to be and run the risk of returning to the traumatic debates which marred their history in the late 1970s and early 1980s.

In electoral terms the problem is more acute and the questions more difficult to tackle. If the party is experiencing a dissipation of its social constituency, is this necessarily a consequence of the emergence and ascendancy of the New Labour project? Would further 'reform', or a reformulation and development of the same project, encourage a greater number of people to return to voting Labour or would it instead only increase the rate of diminution? By contrast, would a sudden move to the left and a return to a modern form of the traditional Labour Party necessarily recoup the lost votes? Although the collapse of Labour's social constituency was certainly concomitant with the zenith of New Labour, it is far from clear whether the process which delivered a more volatile electorate is reversible. It is almost a case not only of asking how to put the toothpaste back in the tube but of determining whether it is in fact possible at all.

Liberal Democrats

In a speech to Liberal Democrat MPs on 24 March 2005 Charles Kennedy declared that in the impending election there were 'no limits' to his party's ambitions. While their aspirations may be unbounded, it is clear that there is nevertheless a very real barrier to the realisation of their goals. The Liberal Democrats are gaining support but the distribution of their electoral success has prevented them from gaining the seats which they need to make the sizeable difference to British politics that they desire. The polling data suggests, in fact, that they are hitting a glass ceiling.

The problem for the Liberal Democrats is how to make the massive leap forwards that would enable them to translate Kennedy's noble sentiments into political reality. As with the Labour Party, this is difficult in two different respects. At a tactical and electoral level the Liberal Democrats must decide whether they wish to focus their attention on providing an alternative source of opposition to the Conservatives or to concentrate on making inroads into Labour's former social constituency. If they direct themselves towards the Conservatives, they risk alienating the support they gained in the north, whereas if they confine themselves to poaching from Labour, they must brace themselves for a long and possibly fruitless journey. At a party-political level this problem is manifested in a similar way to Labour's own conundrum. Determining how to proceed from this juncture involves a very serious consideration of their political alignment. No one would deny that this is a dangerous and difficult cleft in which to be caught. The Liberal Democrats are, after all, a party of political alliance and as such consist of two distinct and occasionally contra-dictory traditions of political philosophy. On the one hand, there are those whose opinions owe most to the liberal roots of the party. In electoral terms this group are best placed to oppose the Conservatives. On the other hand, there are those who are at heart social democrats. These MPs and activists are undoubtedly better placed to bring the party's strategic focus on to challenging Labour, being an historical offshoot of that same party. To date the party as a whole has been able to contain the conflicts between these two wings and has preserved peace through the gradual acquisition of new seats since the merger of the SDP and the Liberals on 3 March 1988. As debate about the way in which to break through the glass ceiling accelerates in the aftermath of the 2005 election, however, these tensions will be brought to the fore and in turn will become difficult to restrain. The party's real problem is therefore how it should go about reconsidering its political orientation without tearing itself apart in the process.

Conservatives

The Conservative Party has been very much the 'quiet man' of the story so far. This is perhaps not undeserved. At the 2005 election the Conservatives failed to increase their national share of the vote and gained only a small number of seats through an incontrovertible swing to their cause. In many, such as Shrewsbury & Atcham, Scarborough & Whitby, Wellingborough, Shipley and Lancaster & Wyre, their success owes more to gains made by the Liberal Democrats from Labour than anything else. In the seats that they retained, although there were some notably increased majorities, the general picture was of continuity with little change. Like the other two major parties, the Conservatives are therefore looking to make gains. Unlike the others, however, their problem is somewhat more pressing. As Labour support declines, the Conservatives naturally have aspirations to government in the near future. Nevertheless they are faced with the unpleasant possibility that should they fail to make sufficient gains at the next election, a Labour party without an absolute majority could be kept in government with the assistance of the Liberal Democrats. Unless they are able to seize enough seats, the Liberal Democrat–Labour alliance that was discussed by Tony Blair and Paddy Ashdown both before and after the 1997 election could be revived.

The Conservatives' problem is that they lack a clear identity and a defined basis for popular appeal. As a party they have been searching for this sense of identity since Margaret Thatcher's resignation and certainly since John Major's defeat at the 1997 election. Now, with Labour obviously facing future difficulties at the polls, their quest is all the more important. The choice over direction, however, is difficult and confused. But it is not so much the tactical and electoral dimension that is the source of complexity as the philosophical dimension. As politicians and activists, Conservatives have always regarded themselves as something of a breed apart, as a unique feature of the political landscape. Yet, while they are certain that they are committed to Conservatism, few are certain what sort of Conservatism they are committed to or, indeed, what Conservatism itself should mean in the twenty-first century. Partly this problem is a consequence of the party's history. Some individuals feel themselves drawn to the party's 'one nation' past and its undertones of duty and social responsibility; others are drawn, if not to Thatcherism per se, then to its strong emphasis on economic credibility and the desire to encourage business growth and enterprise through greater freedom in all areas. Although these strands of thought are all identifiably 'Conservative' in origin, their respective logical conclusions are in many senses highly contradictory. The question therefore becomes a matter of how Conservative politicians foresee their different varieties of 'Conservatism' being specific enough to give the party new direction but broad enough to conserve the integrity of the wider party.

Minor parties
One of the incidental effects of the collapse in Labour's social constituency and the corresponding increase in electoral volatility has been to create what appears to be a greater field of opportunity for minor parties. At the 2005 election three MPs were elected for fringe parties or on an independent platform – George Galloway (Respect, Bethnal Green & Bow), Richard Taylor (Independent Kidderminster Hospital and Health Concern, Wyre Forest) and Peter Law (Independent, Blaenau Gwent) – and a surprising number of small groups won an impressive proportion of the vote. Across the country, the UK Independence Party, the British National Party (BNP), the Green Party and Veritas achieved impressive results and even succeeded in supplanting major parties from their position in certain constituencies.

For the minor parties, each of which has to be considered separately, the problem is slightly different. While Labour, the Liberal Democrats and the Conservatives have to address the issue of how to increase or hold their electoral base through internal change, the minor parties are faced with the problem of whether their opportunity for future development actually exists. Each of the parties must consider why and how it managed to achieve its successes (variously measured) and whether its platform has a long-term future. Of all the parties, the minor parties are confronted with the most specifically electoral problem. Moreover, from an historical perspective, they are obliged to ask whether the origins of their existence have created the opportunity for them to distinguish themselves as distinct political entities. In this sense, the problem is electoral but with the added complications provided by their position as historical aberrations. On the one hand, are the parties of protest actually possessed of a capacity for longevity? On the other hand, are single-issue parties – even where they have broadened their scope, as in the case of the BNP – able to act as anything other than as a magnet for protest and dissent?

2

The Labour Party, triangulation and the politics of the centre

Shortly before the 2005 election I attended a policy briefing at a regional Labour Party conference. A small number of delegates had locked themselves away in a stuffy room for an hour to debate the government's foreign agenda. Three sub-ministers explained their policies in great detail, poring over colourful bar charts and violent scatter graphs to illustrate terrorist outrages and the government's response. I began to notice a certain restlessness amongst some of my comrades. One minister proudly told us the precise figure spent on rebuilding schools in Iraq. A murmur of disquiet passed through the room and a few beads of sweat trickled noiselessly down several faces. After an agonising pause I gingerly raised my hand and enquired, as a candidate for Parliament, what I should say to any member of the public that might cannily ask why we blew them up in the first place. One minister turned an exotic shade of purple, while another looked as though he might cry. I took the ensuing punishment like a man and upon bursting in to the outside fresh air was rewarded with a couple of nervous pats on the shoulder. I had spoken as a lone voice in the wilderness, dry and cracking after a heavy few hours of cheap white wine and soggy canapés. Although the isolated sound of a few tumbleweeds passing by me was unnerving, I sensed that my comrades were privately glad that anybody had spoken at all.

Upon reflection, the meeting was a microcosm of the 2005 campaign and the state the Labour Party has found itself in. The government is enacting policy contrary to its most hallowed traditions, private investment and management in public utilities and unilateral military action being the chief culprits. The members knew it. They were angry and wanted to say something, but were instead choosing to bite their tongue. Election night 2005 was not just philosophically confused, it was downright boring. We drank our leisure centre gin, cheered a few notable decapitations and slunk off to the bar at regular intervals to moan about the lack of facilities for smokers. The results were unengaging and confusing. Every activist knew Tony Blair was going to go soon and harboured a secret passion to do something terrible to him with a potato peeler. But still we pinned on our rosettes, unfurled the posters and campaigned for his re-election. Moreover, no one knew quite what was going to happen next. Somewhere between the bombing of Kabul and the flattening of Baghdad, the party's engine had silently spluttered to a stop. The Blair project was dead. But the carcass of the driver was still at the steering wheel, gathering flies.

Disquiet has not been exclusive to the party. The previous chapter demonstrated that cracks are appearing in the electoral coalition that has sustained past Labour governments. Doubtless this is in part a reflection of long term socio-economic changes among voters, some now too rich to vote Labour and some too poor to bother to vote at all. But we have also demonstrated that much of the shift took place between 1997 and 2005, implying that defection from Labour has been, at least in part, a response to government policy. That defection has been greatest among those that have associated themselves with the party's radical image and socialistic values, notably the long-term unemployed and voters in the North-East and the Celtic fringe. The concern of this chapter is what the impact of Blair's political strategy has been for the Labour Party and, if it can be demonstrated that it has been largely negative, what hope there lies for the creation of alternatives.

A multitude of tensions exist within the Labour Party and on occasion they can bubble quietly to the surface. At the 2004 conference the media's attention was grabbed by a lukewarm resolution to withdraw troops from Iraq. But it missed altogether a passionate floor debate over a proposition to renationalise the railways without compensation. The motion was a reflection of the spirit of a deal struck between the government and union leaders at a policy forum held earlier that year at Warwick University and was carried with a clear majority. Yet the government denounced the motion as being 'ideologically motivated' and its prescription outdated. Conference organisers attempted to use heavy-handed political bargaining to affect delegates' votes and the presiding chair even tried to claim that a motion passed by a sea of hands was 'really very close' before being forced to take an official tally and a secret ballot. Conference passed this landmark resolution, the first time it had endorsed the nationalisation of a public utility for eight years, with 64 per cent voting for public ownership.

Interestingly and unusually, the rift lay not between the front bench and the wider party but between the government and its working-class base in the unions. A breakdown of the vote showed that only a narrow majority of constituency delegates voted for the motion; it was overwhelmingly opposed by unions and affiliated organisations. These patterns of support were reproduced in the 2005 conference fights over council house provision, the role of the private sector in health provision and, most dramatically, secondary picketing. In the floor battle over the right to strike the Prime Minister's office released a statement that warned that the unions were out of step 'not only with MPs . . . but also constituency parties'. This is historically perverse. Throughout the troubled era of the 1970s and 1980s, the leadership relied upon the block votes of the unions to defeat leftist motions from the constituencies. One can infer from the 2004 conference that while the unions are growing restive, the constituency left are slowly disengaging from the conference process altogether. Indeed, in 2004 just under half of all constituencies did not bother to send a voting delegate at all. For the first time in history the root of faction lies with the unions and not at all with the constituencies. This may reflect the decline of the latter, their shrinking membership indicated by the election to conference of large numbers of professional politicians (councillors, party chairs) more likely to be at one with government policy, unlike grassroots activists. The media ignored the fate of the 2004 resolution on the future of the railways and of an earlier one at the same conference to protect council housing stock from privatisation, again backed largely by the unions. It could not be blamed for doing so. A vote at conference, even if it reflects the will of the party, has no guarantee of becoming party policy. The morning after the successful passing of the resolution Gordon Brown, ostensibly the darling of the unions, gracefully dismissed it in a radio interview.

Labour's identity was once brightly coloured by its socialist doctrine and its blue-collar voting base. Cohesion in the past was rare and there has always been a tension between those who see Labour as a party of socialist transformation and those who see it as a party of capitalist democratic government by socialist principles. This debate came to the fore in the late 1970s during the period dubbed as the 'crisis of capitalism'. High unemployment was matched with high inflation to create 'stagflation' and Labour had to navigate its way through a sea of elaborate industrial unrest and wafer-thin parliamentary majorities. This period was considerably more tumultuous than Blair's but it was also considerably more interesting. Labour divided into those that sought to manage the crisis in such a way that would protect Labour's economic constituency and those that wanted to take the opportunity to push through a radical transformation of capitalism. Arguably there are many similarities between Blair and the Prime Minister of fin de siècle socialism, James Callaghan. However, the intellectual climates of their governments were remarkably different and any comparison would be at best superficial. The internal debates of the late 1970s were all conducted within the context of an agreed predominance of the discourse of democratic socialism. All agreed that the function of government was to facilitate the extension of democratic principles to economics. This was a fundamentally materialist doctrine in that it recognised that economics impacted upon people's behaviour. Only by reforming the economic structure of society could the Labour movement free people from poverty and the rigid British class structure and create a happy society. For the left this meant workers' control of factories, mass nationalisation and reform of the constitution. For the right of the party, getting a Labour government elected was both the means and the end. The working class would govern in its own interests and money that individual workers lost through increasing tax rates and inflation would be compensated for by extension of the welfare state.

It is important to stress that this age-old conflict within the party could have resulted in a victory for either element. In the early 1980s the left made a number of significant advances. Tony Benn ran for the parliamentary deputy leadership and nearly won, an electoral college was established to elect the leadership, mandatory reselection was introduced to weed out right-wing MPs and a prominent role in the writing of the manifesto was briefly negotiated. The victory of the right was in part an historical accident. Neil Kinnock was elected by the party as a candidate of the hard left and surprised his critics by turning rightwards. Whether or not a left-wing victory would have destroyed the party electorally is immaterial. What matters is that the party was capable of providing alternatives to its own government's policy framed in the context of its socialist principles. Throughout this bitter struggle Labour was still guaranteed a core of support from the British electorate. This was mainly because large sectional interests within the British population still looked upon Labour governments and ideology as being most capable of providing material improvement or security. Certain legislative commitments, for instance preserving the welfare state, full employment or racial equality, created a coalition of those with a stake in socialism.

New Labour is unconcerned with rebalancing the structure of power in modern Britain. It increases funding for some public projects, such as education and the NHS. But equal access to public services does not make a commitment to redistribution. Instead the government has focussed on reducing 'relative poverty – the gap between the poorest and the typical (median) income . . . We stress that it is not enough to look at absolute poverty – we can't allow the poorest to fall behind.' Although this is a highly admirable approach, it has not created a more equal society. It does not aim to. For instance, between 1998 and 1999 the weekly income of the richest tenth of the population rose by 4 per cent to £560, but the poorest saw a rise of just 1.8 percent to £136. In 2005 the poorest fifth of households possessed just 6 per cent of national income after tax; the richest fifth have enjoyed a rise from 44 per cent to 45 per cent of national income.

This contrasts starkly with the apparent aims of the party of Callaghan. Evidence for this can be found in the 1979 Labour manifesto. This document was not a product of the party membership or hard left activists. Rather it was written by the Prime Minister, his closest Cabinet colleagues and a coterie of the right of the parliamentary party. Indeed, so limited was its authorship that many on the left blamed their general election defeat on its lack of radicalism. Nonetheless it regarded 'prosperity for all' as an egalitarian creed, not just a happy potential by-product of a meritocratic society. Despite being penned by the parliamentary right it stated:

> The Labour Party is a democratic socialist party and proud of it. Labour seeks to build a stronger and more prosperous Britain – and we are determined to see that all our people share fully in that prosperity. We want a Britain which is open and democratic and which puts fair earnings for working people and the needs of the under-privileged before the demands of private profit.

Economic growth was not simply an end in itself but a means to transform working-class people's lives. Not only would its manifesto pledges end absolute poverty but economic growth would be accompanied by (and largely pay for, or justify) increased industrial democracy. Put crudely, economic expansion would allow workers to gain greater control of the means of production and even afford them the right to produce a little less. It is instructive to note that in 2005 Gordon Brown warned conference delegates that he would not strictly enforce Europe's legislation supporting a 48-hour week. In 1979 Labour told potential voters that 'if full employment is to be achieved, longer holidays, time off for study, earlier voluntary retirement, and *a progressive move to a 35-hour working week*, must play an increasing role during the 1980s' (emphasis added).

Our immediate concern is to scrutinise the changes that have taken place in the Labour Party since Blair's election as leader in 1994. What they illustrate is the impact of short-term political choices upon the long-term health of the party and political discourse. In the same manner that the Conservative Party has become the prisoner of policy decisions taken over two decades ago, so Blairism may well have placed severe limitations upon the Labour Party's ability to create new policies and carve out an electoral coalition that will produce the kind of parliamentary majorities it has proved dependent upon in the last eight years. Political parties are as subject to hapless accident as any other agent of historical change. Thus what can begin as a simple political process of post-Cold War realignment can result in the creation of a new style and form of government that the party may find impossible to shake off. The first question to ask is why everything has changed so dramatically. What is the process by which this hallowed discourse, bitter but always contextualised by a shared faith in democratic socialism, has ceased to be at the heart of Labour's programme?

Triangulation

Parties can achieve public association with the political centre by two means. Some radically challenge the status quo and upon success move to carve out a new consensus over which they will inevitably enjoy a monopoly. Margaret Thatcher's government achieved this to a certain degree by the mid-1980s. As stagflation declined and the Cold War heated, policies based on nationalisation and disarmament appeared irrelevant and thus radical in the light of a newly fashioned consensus. The Labour Party was no longer favoured by the public to deal with unions, inflation or hot-tempered Argentines. Thatcher moved the centre dramatically to the right by successfully rewriting traditional government policy and then dubbing those who favoured alternative economic policies as a risk to the new consensus and those who had benefited financially from it. The generation of C2 citizens (largely skilled manual labourers) that voted Conservative for the first time in 1979 continued to do so because their radical set of policies, such as cutting taxes and selling council houses, was perceived to have been endorsed only tentatively by Labour, threatening the benefits won. This method of seizing the centre ground relies upon short-term controversy and long-term success.

This first model can create political prisoners of past successes but it has the distinction of being innovative. The alternative process, nowhere near as audacious, of seizing the centre is triangulation, which provides the basis of Blairism. Shying away from providing a revolutionary set of positions, the triangulating party instead begins by pointing to the radicalism of its opponents and appealing to a centre ground of voters, calculated to swing enough seats to obtain a parliamentary majority. These citizens are usually the stakeholders of orthodoxy: the investors in capitalist democracies, whether it be in mortgages or private pensions, that rely upon a stable economy and the protection of the social status quo. The immediate goal of the triangulating party is thus not to redefine the centre ground but to assess where it lies and surreptitiously move into it. Crucially the assessment of where it lies is not based upon an understanding of its position within the ideological spectrum. The centre that the triangulating party seeks is not a fixed point between philosophical opposites such as capitalism and socialism, libertarianism and totalitarianism. Rather it is a point of agreement with the public on what the latter regards the centrist position as being. Where the people feel the centre ground lies on individual issues could in fact be considered by pupils of politics to be on the centre-left or centre-right of the fixed spectrum. In this manner the triangulating party does not seek to 'lead', 'teach' or give 'order' to the people but to accept its analysis and provide good management of public orthodoxy. It wins elections because it is centrist and, by association, concerned not with ideology but good management. It is competent and endowed with penny-pinching compassion. It is thus highly electable.

This is what the Labour Party did in the period 1994–1997. It rejected economic socialism to embrace an unobtrusive and slow-burning Keynesianism. It took a tough line on law and order and benefit fraud and it accepted private investment in public services. It has remained the dominant party of the centre since 1997. In an article in the *Guardian* in January 2005, Alan Milburn spoke candidly of the fashioning of a new consensus:

> New Labour does not just dominate the centre ground; we are reshaping it for progressive purposes . . . A new consensus is being forged and, for the first time in generations, it belongs to progressives. As we seek that historic third term, we seek too a New Labour settlement that locks in progress.

He added, however, 'Having the courage to change our party gave us popular permission to change our country.' In essence he had conceded that Labour's realignment came *before* it was capable of 'reshaping' the centre ground. Triangulation was key to Labour's electoral dominance and the confidence with which Milburn declared that 'progressive purposes' were the new centre ground demonstrates its as yet unabated success.

This model has many obvious short-term benefits. Labour has been able to outmanoeuvre its opponents. A triangulation of policy permits the party to define its opponents as extremist, occupying the fringes of the political spectrum. Other parties attempting to draw distinctions between themselves and the triangulated party inevitably draw distinctions between themselves and what the public perceives to be the moderate opinion. They render themselves apparently unelectable and the triangulated party sweeps to power on the back of its appeal to a reasonable majority. The most successful application of this strategy was the 2001 election. The Labour Party's propaganda effectively dubbed William Hague's Tory Party as extreme, its manifesto going so far as to warn that the Conservatives 'threaten the stability of the UK'. Only 15 per cent of the public preferred Hague to Blair for the top job, the exact percentage that preferred Michael Foot to Thatcher in 1983. Hague was rated as being out of touch with ordinary people by 59 per cent and pluralities of the population felt that the Conservative Party was also 'out of touch' (36 per cent) and 'prepared to promise anything' to get elected (46 per cent). Fewer people told pollsters that it represented all classes and more people than in 1997 responded that they felt it was 'too extreme'. Some 66 per cent felt that the Tories were not prepared for government. Overall the Labour Party was felt to offer the policies more in tune with the public's feelings by 43 per cent, compared with just 22 per cent for the Conservatives. The 2001 election was the high point of Blair's triangulation strategy, winning a historic full second term with a remarkable majority.

However, there are three serious long-term downsides to this electoral model. First, triangulation demands the rejection of value-based politics. By its very definition the triangulating party is prepared to alter any aspect of its policy to match a perceived consensus, devaluing ideology and root principle. This is a particular problem for a socialist party. The Conservatives can alter economic policy without sacrificing ideology because they essentially do not have any. They are instead wedded to cultural values, to patriotism, constitution and community. But a socialist party is defined by its materialist doctrine. Labour has a wider cultural identification, specifically with the labour movement and the ethnic white working class, but its significance is declining in the face of immense economic and social change. In essence, a socialist party is nothing without its ideology. Without ideology one is inclined to ask why a party of the left would bother to run for office at all. For the Labour Party to claim to be a party of management is not just to accept the operations of the free-market system, but to seek to perfect it. Such a philosophy is anachronistic to the Labour movement and its traditions. The question of why Labour does what it does will attain greater significance when its charismatic Prime Minister leaves office. Bereft of personality, it will have to rely upon fear of Conservative victory to energise its activists and voting block. It certainly used fear of the election of Michael Howard to spearhead its campaign in 2005, adopting the slogan 'Britain is working. Don't let the Tories wreck it.' It was even accused of anti-Semitism, in an advert that depicted Howard and Oliver Letwin as flying pigs. Polls regularly reported that the public did not approve of this negativity and rewarded the Liberal Democrats for their apparently positive world-view. A triangulated party runs the risk of being accused of being valueless.

The second by-product of triangulation for any party that previously defined itself by a radical materialist doctrine is the rise in the significance of social policy. When a consensus is formed on economic policy – usually caused by a rejection of structural change by socialist parties – and if there is relative prosperity, the public's attention turns to other matters. Put simply, Labour has shrugged off the radical economics that used to define it, shrinking the electoral distinction between it and the Conservative Party. For the right this is not a problem and can even play to its advantage. A triangulated party of the right such as the Australian Liberal Party can be grateful for the realignment of political significance. During the 2004 Australian elections the Liberal Party was able to successfully campaign almost exclusively on family values and opposition to immigration. However, this focus on social concerns does not bode well for parties of the left.

A prime example of this can be found in Labour's immigration policy. It is a good indicator of the damage triangulation can wreak on both electoral politics and cohesive government. For all the electoral rhetoric of the 2005 election, immigration remains an intractable problem. It is neither possible in practical terms to prevent a certain degree of illegal immigration, nor is it is desirable economically. Wedded as all three main parties are to free-market economics, the discourse over the restriction of labour movement has been left to those parties that desire national control over the economy, such as the British National Party and the Green Party. In fact Labour has been assiduously favourable to the economic migrant, who in turn has been favourable to the UK's service industry boom. Labour has encouraged record levels of entrance to Britain and advocates Turkey's early entry into the European Union. The rise in the significance of immigration to the electorate since 1997 has been proof of the decline in interest in the issues of economic management (inflation and unemployment) due to Labour's concessions to the Thatcherite consensus on economics. Current concern with immigration is not economic but cultural. The modern consensus on mass immigration is that while it guarantees cheap labour for the service economy, it also encourages crime, welfare abuse and social breakdown. According to MORI, the public's concern at the time of the election was not with the economic costs of immigration; 45 per cent felt that it helped Britain's markets. But 36 per cent felt that it had increased crime significantly.

Labour in government was faced with a choice. It could have challenged this consensus by making a radical, progressive case for current immigration levels. The wisdom of its decision not to is unimportant for this chapter. Rather, it is significant that it chose to carve out a 'middle way' on immigration and claim the 'centrist' position for itself. This centrist position is not particularly centrist and most certainly not liberal. It is based not on a coherent philosophy of what a centrist position might be but on simply placing oneself between the other two parties in terms of policy. The result was contradictory, on the one hand declaring, 'The vast bulk of migration . . . is legitimate and welcome as it strengthens our economy and public services.' On the other hand, the 2005 manifesto stated bluntly, 'Our overall

approach will reduce the numbers of people coming into the UK.'
Coherent government policy was being sacrificed in the process of
striking a balance between the Tories and the Liberal Democrats.

As a result of triangulation, boom and Labour's decision to acquiesce
to the Thatcher consensus, there was a notable lack of interest in
economics during the 2005 election. According to MORI, management
of the economy was seventh on the list of people's voting priorities and
unemployment was eleventh. Labour was instead being forced to talk
about policy areas upon which it could not win. Fifty-six per cent said
law and order was the most significant issue in 2005, and 37 per cent
immigration. The problem with increased debate on social issues is that
society is by its very nature conservative; keen to protect its cultural
identity and suspicious of libertarian individualism. The British public
may have appreciated Labour's desire to act tough on immigration but it
suspected that the Conservatives were willing and able to go a little bit
further. According to MORI, immigration and crime were the only
issues on which Michael Howard led Tony Blair among the public. On
the former, 47 per cent felt Howard could be better trusted to tackle
immigration abuse compared with 29 per cent for Blair. Contrasted with
managing the economy (Blair led by 55 per cent to 24 per cent), this
showed a substantial degree of support for Howard, despite the government's tough talk. Moreover the public detected the gap between
government social and economic policy. It may have spoken in doom-
laden terms about immigration during the election but a staggering 65
per cent of the public felt that the government was being flagrantly
dishonest about levels of immigration. As long as it did not threaten to
end in repatriation and yellow stars, the public has historically favoured
the social-policy conventions of the Conservatives. For this reason, on
every one of the social-policy areas debated in the 2005 election the
public favoured the Conservative position.

Meanwhile, on the leftward flank, Labour's refusal to defend
immigration alienated those valuing civil rights and an overtly liberal
agenda. Liberal Democrat campaign material in universities asked its
potential voters how they felt about forced deportations and asylum
centres. Thus triangulation did not entirely play to Labour's favour in
2005. It may have made the government appear reasonable and

competent, but it also rendered it boring and unable to create policy initiatives on the subjects that the public cared about. Moreover, it had assumed that the centre ground on immigration lay with the Conservative agenda of greater control and had tried to adopt this 'centre' as its own. But Labour could never go as far as the Conservatives to satisfy the public's social conservatism and in the process of trying to do so it alienated the left-leaning middle class, who drifted ever further towards the Liberal Democrats. Labour had thrown away a chance to alter the public discourse by championing immigration from 1997 onwards, a policy that many of its spokesmen and certainly its government departments appear to endorse with enthusiasm. The significance of the social issues is not going to decline any time soon. Indeed, fears over terrorism and concern about immigration go hand in hand. After the terrorist bombings of London in July 2005, terrorism rose to the position of the 'most important issue facing Britain today' in polling. Just behind it was immigration, rising from fourth to second place in a matter of days.

The third downside of triangulation is a by-product of the first two. With the rootlessness and fluidity of policy positions comes activist apathy. At the peak of Blair's electoral success the party could boast a membership of 400,000. The current figure is estimated at half that, 40,000 having left since 2001. It could be even lower. In the summer of 2005 the party's national executive debated raising membership subscriptions to cover the overall loss from resignations and defections. The figure quoted as being for lost income if the conference rejected the subscription increase was £1.2 million. From this one can infer that there are currently only 100,000 standard rate-paying members. The party chair, Ian McCartney, blamed constituency organisation, but policy choices seem more likely. A decline in public activism is reflected in dysfunction within the party machine. One Labour Party historian wrote recently of Celtic politics that 'the pulse of the party in Labour's Scottish heartlands is beating ever fainter'. On nomination contests he commented, 'The turnout of members to vote was desultory.' Andrew Coulson, a Birmingham city councillor, writing for Renewal, an internal centre-left organisation, gave a good illustrative account of Labour's activist decline:

The Labour members are demoralised. Ward meetings are barely quorate. New members come and go. Local party members are active as school governors – since political parties are the main means through which 'local authority' governors are recruited. They are less active in residents' associations, neighbourhood forums, or in attending area committees or other decentralised arrangements of the local authority. It is as if they feel that membership of one local organisation, in their case the local party branch, is sufficient.

Many of those still willing to work [in the election] were reluctant – fundamentally disturbed by the war in Iraq, disagreeing with the introduction of private capital into health and education, unconvinced by aggressive law and order and asylum policies promoted by David Blunkett before his resignation as Home Secretary. They were working more for the re-election of their individual MP than to support the front bench . . . But, as national strategies have moved into ground previously occupied by the Conservatives, more and more of the core members feel alienated . . . The grass roots members went along with New Labour in the 1990s, often with reservations, because they could see it was the way to win elections. But now, for many, their party has been taken over by an ideologically driven group with its own agenda. They want it back. If they do not get it, and the omens are not good, we will end up with a national party with a tiny local membership. American politics is already like this.[1]

In the last sentence the author makes a salient point. Blairism is not an entirely British project but one inspired by the experiences of Australasian and American centre-left parties. Even in the most recent election, Blair recruited one of Bill Clinton's top political advisers, Mark Penn, to strategise the campaign. In the US the Democratic Party was long sustained by an economic coalition. Although association with social permissiveness and its dire choice of presidential nominees kept it from holding the most powerful executive office for many years, it was consistently dominant in local and Congressional elections. Clinton won back the presidency at the expense of this dominance. He adopted a strategy of triangulation which gave electors the image of a man juggling both left and right in America's best interests. To quote him:

I had to practice the politics of 'triangulation', bridging the divide between

Republicans and Democrats and taking the best ideas of both. To many liberals and some in the press corps, triangulation was a compromise without conviction; a cynical ploy to win re-election . . . I had always tried to synthesize new ideas and traditional values, and to change government policies as conditions changed.[2]

In so doing he created, or more importantly reined his party to, an economic consensus that demolished the old New Deal coalition established by Roosevelt. He embraced free-trade policies that moved thousands of jobs overseas, outlawed affirmative action within federal hiring and created a 'welfare-to-work' programme that loosened the Democrats' appeal to the poorest in society. He accepted the Republicans' economic agenda and in so doing assisted their aim of moving debate on to social issues, upon which the Christian right was better organised and more enthusiastic. The poorest groups in society generally require motivation to vote because, in an age defined by the dismantling, and to an extent demonisation, of the welfare state, they are without a stake in government. In the past few elections poor American voters have been faced with a choice between Democrats who have dropped their economic populism in favour of grey centrism and a rejuvenated Republican Party with strong, popular Christian values. Consensus on economic liberalism has shifted American political discourse towards the social issues, upon which the Republicans have a natural appeal. In 2000 George W. Bush took the votes of 65 per cent of those that attend church once a week or more. That election marked the beginning of a massive shift of working-class American support from the Democrats to the Republicans, which was accentuated by John Kerry's candidacy four years later. Interestingly, in 2000 Al Gore provided a hint of where Democratic electoral success really lay. At that year's convention the nominee gave a speech in which he called for one of the most radically populist Democratic economic platforms for twenty years. The resultant 'bounce' in the opinion polls was the largest increase for a candidate ever produced by a convention and for a few weeks Gore led Bush. But this was an isolated incident of a successful return to first principles. A fallout among traditionally Democratic voters and activists has proved the rule. In the last two elections the Democrats have failed to carry West Virginia, a state so poor it even voted for Jimmy Carter over Ronald Reagan in 1980. Activism has declined and the numbers of people registering as Democrats has plummeted.

If modern political debate is reduced to an issue of the 'style' rather than the 'substance' of government, then the 2005 election should be a warning to Labour. The public is weary of New Labour and if politics becomes valueless then it is likely to look for an alternative. A MORI poll for the *Observer* at the election found that by clear pluralities on the issues of healthcare, education and personal finances, the public felt certain that things would significantly improve in the next term. For instance, 45 per cent felt that healthcare was going to get much better, 27 per cent that it would stay the same and 20 per cent that it would decline. Yet 56 per cent indicated that they were dissatisfied with the government. Before May 2005 only 32 per cent felt that Blair was inclined to tell the truth on most subjects and on trust Michael Howard consistently led Blair during the election. This reflects the status of polling in the United States on the eve of the 2000 presidential election. The public felt happy, healthy and wise but voted Bush in because they were extremely dissatisfied with the incumbent administration's association with sleaze and corruption. The issue of the 'style of government' could prove to be equally beneficial to the British Conservatives.

What is Blairism?

Triangulation gives the impression that Blair's politics are inherently unprincipled, the product of an age within liberal democracies characterised by parties of both left and right squeezing votes from the centre until the pips squeak. But the process of triangulation has produced a new species of Labour government and its nature demands analysis because it has succeeded like no triangulation movement before or since. Although it might find its practical roots in Australian and American politics, New Labour has become the defining movement of the Middle Way and its admirers. Leaders from Gerhard Schröder of the German Social Democrats to Gennady Zyuganov of the Russian Communist Party have cited Blair as their John the Baptist, rather than

Bill Clinton. Since 1997 Europe has been through a Middle Way revolution. Reformed social democratic parties won power in France and Germany and parties of the right that openly espoused Blairite policies and catchphrases advanced themselves handsomely in Italy and Spain. Since then all those governments that invested political capital in Blairism have been, or are about to be, kicked out of office. Yet Blair has survived two further elections, including a second landslide. The circumstances that made this possible are accounted for throughout this book, but this success is what makes an understanding of Blairism important.

Canny manipulation of the political centre and the contradictory nature of government policy have led some critics to accuse the Labour government and Blairism of being unprincipled and philosophically empty. Cutting away its socialist roots has allowed the government to escape a certain degree of ideological analysis, because most experts have been convinced that Blair has none. He stands accused of operating not out of principle but by the conventions of public debate – or, at worst, by the statistical data provided to No. 10 by 'focus groups'. As a result critics have tended to focus their attacks upon the style of government rather than its substance. Before the 2003 Iraq war popular critiques dealt almost exclusively with the conventions of the Blairite inner circle, eschewing structural analysis for a kind of gossip column familiarity with the personalities behind the throne. Andrew Rawnsley's *Servants of the People* has been one of the most successful of a breed of studies that has explained government policy in terms of an 'obsession with control of the media' and the 'protection of its image'. Rawnsley presents Blairism as a smokescreen for precisely nothing at all and its civil service a casting couch for advertising executives. Behind the Wizard's curtain sits not a wizened old man but a glorified door-to-door salesman with a degree in politics from the LSE.

Even after Iraq most critics continued to blame policy errors on Blair's style of government. This represented an ungenerous refusal to believe that Blair could have made such a profound political mistake out of conviction. The Cabinet quitters Clare Short and Robin Cook both argued that the war was a product of Blair's style of government. It was driven by the vanity of one man who wanted a place in history as the liberator of Baghdad. Cabinet has ceased to function as a scrutiniser of policy and a forger of a collective will and, combined with a lobotomised civil service appointed by the government from within the Labour Party, has become a rubber stamp. Cook and Short explained their belated resignations as evidence of the total control of information by No. 10. Thus a direct link can be made between Rawnsley's analysis that the paranoid government had erected a cocoon to protect itself from the media, creating a 'government within a government', to Cook and Short's protests about the inability to protest. The war was the ultimate indicator of the failings in the Blair style of government. Short stated, 'There is no real collective responsibility because there is no collective – just diktats in favour of increasingly badly thought through policy initiatives that come from on high.'[3]

In order to protect their own reputations many ex-Cabinet members have rewritten history. Short's claim that the war was the culmination of a crisis induced by a style of government is erroneous. It is impossible to believe that she did not notice the patterns in British foreign policy that began to play out as soon as she entered office in 1997. To suggest that Britain went to war on a whim devoid of a philosophy of government is to ignore the interventions in Serbia, Sierra Leone and Afghanistan. Similarly Frank Dobson's claim to the TUC in 2003 that 'foundation hospitals and private treatment centres would spell the end of the NHS' seems disingenuous when one considers that PFI was first experimented with when he was Secretary of State for Health in 1997.

This would imply that it is not style but substance that is responsible for the state Labour is in. Policy continuity within Blairism is evident, which creates a tension among its critiques. For Clinton and his right-wing Democratic Leadership Conference, the Third Way represents a long-term cultural commitment to conservatism (most members of the DLC are from the south), and for many on the old right of the British Labour Party it was a means of gaining office. But some Blairites take it as an article of faith that the Third Way actually stands for something. If in terms of strategy it is a response to post-Cold War social changes, then in principle and ideology it is too. The Third Way is part of a wider search for answers in the post-Cold War world; it asks quite simply: why should we care? Even if the politics of the last seven years has been fashioned by electoral expediency, Blair's vanguard has tried to answer just that question, either out of principle or to justify themselves. One rhetorical, thematic justification of its policy has been the much vaunted concept of 'social justice'. By this one might assume that the government is tapping into the language of the Labour Party of the past, a language steeped in the discourse of human rights. For instance, under the subheading 'The penal system' the authors of the 1983 election manifesto wrote, 'No one concerned for human dignity and civil rights can find our prison system acceptable. We are determined to improve conditions.' It is impossible to imagine such a line appearing in a modern manifesto of frankly any mainstream party.

In strong contrast New Labour's understanding of government is based on the principles of a new social contract: society favours those that play by a collectively agreed set of rules. Provision is based upon responsibility and contract to authority. It is not a recognition of one's inalienable human rights. The 2005 manifesto was framed by these ideas. To quote Alan Milburn:

> [Our reforms] comprise a new contract between state and citizen, where government provides opportunities and people strive to take them. If people put something in, they get something back. This is the means to rebalance rights and responsibilities; to reward effort and enterprise; to reclaim for progressive purposes the banner of ambition and aspiration. And it is the means to reconnect with hard-working people, middle- and low-income alike – who want to know there are fair rules in play, and there is a government on their side.[4]

This was reflected in the election manifesto, which told the reader, 'Labour will go forward with our plans for ID cards to tackle crime and welfare abuse . . . Forward to a fair deal for those that play by the rules, not back to a raw deal.' This statement is of great significance. It demonstrates the social-contract nature of New Labour's policies, that they are based around a collective notion of playing by the rules. The term 'social justice' is, perhaps, a little misleading.

From this one can infer that Labour has totally rejected a structural analysis of the problems facing British society. It rejects the view that people are imprisoned in economic and social structures, for instance that people commit crime because of poverty, upbringing or alienation from society. One can make a good link with the popular philosophy that abounded in the 1990s of Third Way thought, particularly that expounded by Anthony Giddens. His concept of 'structuration' was really a compendium of many thinkers who attempted to construct a poststructural analysis of how and why society functions. He argued that people are 'knowledgeable' and that their everyday sociological knowledge feeds into their behaviour. They have reasons for doing what they do. Consequently, sociology should not be used as an excuse to explain behaviour as due to 'society'. People are responsible for their actions and social democratic politics should embrace that fact. This view has, on the one hand, certainly allowed the Labour Party to adopt some liberating policies and encourage greater choice and freedom of economic movement. On the other hand, the proposition is conservative in that it assumes that the rules by which society regulates itself are correct and rejects the idea that people might seek to break them because of economic or social imbalance. People understand the actions they take and the consequences they produce; they are not prisoners of economic structure as Labour's previous materialist doctrine held them to be.

The 2005 manifesto took such thought to its logical extreme and buried Labour's materialism: 'Our next step is to revive the idea of community policing for the modern world – targeting the offender and not just the offence.' It identified the roots of crime as 'drug and alcohol misuse, and the lack of respect for community'. It did not discuss why these problems occur in the first place. The manifesto makes no connection between economics and crime. In the 1983 manifesto, the section on crime and communities stated, 'We will act to ensure, through the policies set out in this campaign document, that people living in the inner cities have access to decent homes, health and education – and that there is proper accountability for the police.' A Labour-sponsored publication placed the blame for rising crime rates firmly on the shoulders of ministers whose policies created unemployment: 'If boys and girls do not obtain jobs when they leave school, they feel that society has no need for them . . . Unemployment leads to poorer social conditions, even broken families, and it is these factors which lead some of those affected to become involved in crime.'

New Labour's emphasis upon the individual's responsibility towards his community may well be entirely politically motivated, a response to growing social conservatism among the voting public. It is also representative of the philosophical evolution of only a section of the New Labour elite. Nonetheless, any further doubts as to Labour's embrace of Tory principles are easily quashed by the front bench's constant appeals to the support of wet Conservatives. In an article with the sub-heading 'Labour's values in a modern context', Milburn actually attributed his values to one-nation Toryism: 'As we advance to the next election, we need to rebuild the coalition around "one nation politics" that recognises while life is hard for many, all should have the chance to succeed; where, if you play by the rules, you get a chance to progress.'

In the 2005 election Milburn did not just hope that his Labour values might appeal to floating wet Tory voters. He was actually claiming that his party's philosophy was wet Toryism. Thus, in the last few years, Blairism has been developing its own rationale, independent from the traditions of its party's philosophy and electoral coalition. If this is the case then it is likely to fall foul of the negatives of triangulation already addressed. If Labour is preparing for a debate on collective responsibility, tough policing, immigration controls and social authoritarianism, it should be warned that it is a battle the polls indicate that the Tories are most likely to win. In the process of fighting it, it has shrugged off its socialistic roots and an understanding of society based on a critique of capitalism and a human-rights discourse. Whether or not it is capable of returning to those roots is worth considering.

Strategies for renewal

This book is concerned with the problems of the current political discourse. Within the Labour Party one finds the microcosm of the modern political system and within it evidence of the structural faults that currently prevent the formation of alternative policies and new ideas. Put simply, in the last twenty years the Labour Party's internal structure of democracy has been emasculated to such an extent that one must consider it virtually impossible both to construct a formidable alternative to Blairism and to turn it into government policy. That this has occurred is demonstrated by the lack of any serious challenge to Tony Blair's leadership. It is true that there have been a growing number of parliamentary rebellions against Blair. But they do not represent one serious, co-ordinated effort. They have not been lead by a charismatic, alternative parliamentary leadership. They have not operated under the aegis of a coherent grouping: only the Socialist Campaign Group regularly meets to discuss tactics and its membership is small and rapidly ageing. Perhaps most importantly, they have not tagged on to heavy-weight figureheads with some role or authority within the Cabinet.

Instead, Parliament has seen largely atomised rebellions, lacking in clear philosophical direction, lashing out at individual policies that step over marks that are not clearly delineated by ideology. They are increasing in their number and their reporting, but they remain tiny. It is true that there is now a backbench rebellion in roughly one of every three divisions, but they are all pitifully small and are dominated by familiar old faces. On one sample night in November 2005, the party whip was defied on two occasions over a government-sponsored Bill. This may seem frequent, but the first saw only one MP rebel, the second only four. Between May and November 2005 (before the debate on terrorist detentions) thirty-six Conservative MPs defied the whip, compared with sixty-three Labour, representing almost equal proportions of their parliamentary membership (18.2 per cent for the Conservatives, 17.7 per cent for Labour). Admittedly this situation may change when Labour's majority shrinks, as its rebels tend to come from safe seats and its loyalists from marginal ones. It is undeniable that Blair's back benches are considerably more restive than ever before, but in many regards this is evidence of how uncomfortably his leadership and policies have sat with a significant rump of MPs from a variety of ideological backgrounds. As the majority gets smaller, so the party's Blairite leadership will have to negotiate with a parliamentary membership that comes from backgrounds and seats not entirely partial to Blairism. Nonetheless it is unlikely that a dynamic alternative to Blairism will be crafted by his back benches.

It is true that internal opposition to Blair has been suffocated by massive majorities that have previously hidden the scale and potential impact of parliamentary dissent over government policy. One might speculate on the impact of a smaller victory in 1997 upon public-service reform or even the war in Iraq. Equally it is true that Blair's electoral success, coming in the wake of eighteen years of opposition, has also blunted the attacks of the hard left. But, put into an historical context, these explanations are simply not good enough. Harold Wilson enjoyed a large parliamentary majority from 1966 to 1970, but his premiership was called into regular question in Parliament and even within his own Cabinet. Not only were his Cabinet opposition respected political heavyweights whose regularly threatened resignations carried the seal of potential political turmoil but they also represented ideological factions within the wider party and were felt to be able to call upon sections of Parliament and party to support them: James Callaghan the trade unions, Barbara Castle the Tribune/soft Left and Roy Jenkins the Lib-Lab Europhiles. With the exception of Gordon Brown, no such towering figures exist within the Cabinet today and certainly none can claim to speak for sectional interests. Those that have disapproved of government policy have simply resigned and, as they have done so, there has been no threat of the Prime Minister following them. If the claims regarding Blair's treatment of Brown's political ambitions are even remotely true, then he has shown in comparison with his 1960s forebears the patience of a saint in refusing to resign or call a leadership contest. Either his disquiet with Blair's leadership is exaggerated or he too realises the impossibilities of open dissent.

The latter possibility indicates that the greatest significant structural change is within the party itself. Throughout its post-war history, the left opposition has been the catalyst of ideological renewal, both proposing Marxist policies for fledgling manifestos and encouraging the parliamentary right to drum up their own alternatives to deflect charges of philosophical stagnation. Their views may have often slipped the moorings of sanity, but the left did force the party to reconsider its constitution twice after 1945, the second occasion resulting in the electoral college for election of the leadership and a reselection process for MPs. The latter was used to almost deselect the Blairite MP Oona

King in 2004, shortly before her constituents chose to. The hard left was the New Politics of the 1980s. It laid many of the foundations for social policies that would later become de rigueur for the Blair government. They introduced all-women shortlists, fought racism within the party and promoted alternative lifestyles. Moreover, many of the current Blairites campaigned for Tony Benn in the deputy leadership competition of 1981, chief among them Blair himself, Alan Milburn and Harriet Harman. Rebellions in Parliament, then, are isolated and useless if they are not linked with mass disobedience within the party, as they were in the 1980s. And the silence of the Labour Party left since 1997 is historically unique. Considering the flagrantly rightist nature of some policies, such as ID cards and the renewal of the Trident nuclear arsenal, it is remarkable.

The silence of the party was achieved by two means. The first was cultural. The creation of the terms 'New' and 'Old' Labour have simply spelled the end of the Labour left. The terms are of course absurd in any context other than chronology. Nationalisation of major industries and public services is 'Old' in the sense that it was last carried out in 1979. However its death as proposed government policy is relatively recent, given that in 1997 Blair promised to take the national grid 'back into the public's hands'. Similarly, withdrawal from the EU is 'Old' in that it is no longer in the manifesto, but then it has not been so since 1983, a good eleven years before all the Newness kicked in. It seems churlish to dub a policy as 'Old' simply because it's been out of circulation for a while (unilateral invasions taste strongly of old chestnuts, after all) but the significance of the use of the adjective 'Old' cannot be overstressed. It has reduced all debate over policy direction to a discourse of socialism versus modernity, old versus new. This makes a future reversal of policy unlikely. It makes it easy to (often inaccurately) characterise those who oppose government reforms as 'conservative', as offering no concrete alternative policies and simply voting to protect the interests of key constituent groups. MPs that have opposed private finance initiatives, literacy hours and public employee cutbacks can be easily dismissed as union voice-pieces. In this manner Labour's left runs the risk of becoming like its US Democratic counterpart, which is consistently labelled as the tool of 'special interests', preserving the status quo for those that currently benefit from it.

The second means of achieving party obedience was structural. The old Clause 4 was introduced by Arthur Henderson and Sydney Webb in 1918 specifically to dampen the revolutionary spirit within the Labour Party. At the same time as Henderson reordered the constitution to shift power away from the trade unions at conference, so Webb wrote a defining statement of doctrine that was notable by its refusal to define anything at all. The significance of its rewriting in 1995 was immense. The old clause, while woolly, did commit Labour to the principle of democratic control over the economy, its goal being 'to secure for the producers by hand or by brain the full fruits of their industry'. With the rewriting, the Blairites altered the discourse within the party for the foreseeable future. The left could no longer argue that in campaigning for either syndicalism or workers' control they were demanding the party stay true to its own constitution. They have had to shift their case away from a complete, constitutional overhaul of government policy and towards incremental socialist reforms, for they are no longer the guardians of Labour's ideology.

This has resulted in a proliferation of special-interest groups campaigning within the party on individual issues, symptomatic of a wider Balkanisation of the left. Socialism used to act not only as an umbrella but also as a lightning rod for minority campaigns. Gay, black, feminist and environmental activists may have devoted their energies to a particular cause within socialism, but they considered themselves part of the same movement, regardless of the awkward bedfellows they courted. During the 1984 miners' strike a group called Lesbians Against Pit Closures was formed. It maintained strong links with the mining community of Dulais, south Wales. Exchange visits were arranged and benefits organised, the money collected going to support striking miners and their families. But now socialism and its adherents are simply one of many special interests competing for space within the manifesto. Arguably they always were, but today they have a diminishing claim to represent Labour values. As a result they have no inherent right to force the government to explain and reassess itself in any ideological light at all. The party's leadership and ideologues are speaking different languages and neither understands the other.

Moreover, any group that tries to campaign for a change to government policy faces a number of obstacles that make it almost impossible to effect that change. The powers of Conference have been limited enormously. The party's governing National Executive Council has been rebalanced away from spaces being given to elected members, so that taking a position upon it has limited importance, and consultation exercises have replaced the resolutions that previously formed government policy. These obstacles were not all set up exclusively by Blair. Neil Kinnock's assault on the Trotskyite Militant Tendency in the 1980s has cast a long shadow over groups attempting to organise a challenge to front bench power. The ban on Militant laid down a number of definitions of anti-party behaviour that render organisation simply impossible. Any group attempting to co-ordinate dissent can be declared a party within a party if it attempts to discipline its own membership. This precludes entryism from the Labour Party. Any group attempting to construct a broad doctrinal approach to challenging the leadership will have to discipline its own membership if it has to have coherency and organisation.

In summary, it is now inconceivable that what used to be the vanguard of radical policy change, the left, could ever facilitate a rethinking of party policy. The structure for confrontation, bargaining and the collective formation of policy is gone, rendering the left impotent. Neither is it helped by parliamentary democracy. Britain lacks the structure by which groups within parties can appeal over the heads of their leadership to the nation at large. In the US, where the parties have primaries, a left- or right-leaning Democrat could gain credibility by running against their party's establishment and garnering an impressive number of votes. Ordinary citizens can vote in elections without party membership and Democrat can run against Democrat. Thus in 1968 Eugene McCarthy was able to alter Democratic Party foreign policy for the next eight years by campaigning on a leftist platform and winning a number of primaries. A radical candidate in Britain has first to gain nomination by campaigning amongst a small number of activists, limiting his legitimacy, and upon election he does not gain an executive office of significance but is subsumed within a legislative body. The closest the government has come to a challenge from within its own ranks was from Ken Livingstone. But his challenge ended in defection, which made him unpopular with the national party. His eventual return to Labour was not wholly a sign of his victory; it was unlikely that he could have run a second campaign for the London mayoralty without the party's funds and doorstep activism. Indeed, it indicates that left-wing politicians will for the foreseeable future rely upon the Labour Party's money and structure. It is no surprise that the radical Labour groups of the 1980s spoke of extra-parliamentary democracy and pinned their hopes on Arthur Scargill's miners and the Liverpool councillors rather than the Labour Party leadership.

One has to conclude that the chance of a revival of grassroots or parliamentary political alternatives to front bench policy within the Labour Party is nil. Not only is this situation historically unusual, it is also deeply frustrating for contemporary activists, particularly as the remaining elements of the Labour coalition are becoming radicalised. Labour members played a significant role in the Stop the War Coalition. A number of trade unions have elected neo-Marxist executive boards and some have made overtures to the Liberal Democrats. With the approach of a leadership competition one would expect the mass membership of the party to be able to exact demands and renew its leadership's commitment to ideology. But there is no evidence that such a thing is taking place. Therefore any future change of Labour Party policy will have to be constructed outside the language of socialism and very probably outside the party structure altogether.

Stuck in the middle with whom?

In July 2005 Patricia Hewitt, the Secretary of State for Health, gave a speech entitled 'Labour's values and the modern NHS'. She told the audience that she was giving the talk in response to a confrontation with a former comrade in which she had been asked, 'How does it feel to go from feminist campaigner to champion of the private sector in the NHS?' The deeply leaning question illustrated the old left's capacity to unite radical campaigns under one ideological banner, implying that feminism was at one time synonymous with nationalisation. Her reply neatly summarised the process of electoral and ideological realignment in 1997 that eight years later created a bastardised ideology, leaving rootlessness and confusion in its wake. With the zeal of a convert she confessed her previous sins as a socialist: 'I remember very clearly our disastrous opposition to the sale of council houses. We thought we were opposing the sale of a public asset; council tenants realised we were denying them the chance . . . to buy their own home.' The same was true of the modern NHS. She proposed reform to her audience because she detected that the public demanded it, not because it was in accordance with their socialist values. 'It would be a major mistake – a mistake the Conservatives are just waiting for us to make – to deny people choices over their health and healthcare, leaving us out of step with irreversible changes in society and out of touch with the people we seek to serve.'

This is triangulation in practice. Hewitt muted any potential opposition by slipping in to the classic Labour discourse of Old versus New:

> It is much easier to go on doing things the way they've always been done. Much easier not to reconfigure services . . . Much easier – at least in the short term until the deficits build up, the waiting lists start to grow up, and people who can afford it go elsewhere and those who can't are left behind.

This ignored the reality that her major internal opposition does not propose that things stay the same at all. Unison argues for a range of alternatives to public-sector funding, including using direct taxation or public-sector bonds to pay for hospital buildings. Hewitt's comments on past Labour policies also smacked of rewriting history. 'Old' Labour did not oppose council house ownership, but insisted that whether or not it should happen be decided by balloting affected estates and that the resultant profits should go straight in to new housing stock.

But most strikingly, the speech was full of intellectual inconsistencies and evidence of the whittling down of old values into sound-bites. 'We are a progressive party', she declared, 'and our goal should be to democratise choice. We want to spread individual choice and build collective voice in the NHS.' Precisely how New Labour could wed individualism and the introduction of market reforms with collectivism passed unexplained. The language of the past was being used uncomfortably to explain away the inconsistencies of the present. 'We know, as modern social democrats, that dynamic, open and competitive markets are the best way to produce most goods and services, to generate employment and create wealth.' In sum, the secretary of state was proposing a bold initiative to reintroduce internal markets. The primary care trusts she was promoting would be permitted to accept competing bids from a range of private providers.

The future does not look bright for the New Labour project. The short-term success of triangulation has created long-term structural problems for the renewal of Labour's electoral appeal. The party has alienated the coalition of voters that have supported it in the past and has spread mass disaffection amongst its membership. It has severed its connection with that past, creating a valueless future. It has shifted political debate away from those issues upon which it scores highly among the public and towards those issues upon which the Conservatives are considered capable of the kind of radical reform the public favours. It has been the victim of its own success. Moreover, one cannot see any hope for a renewal of Labour's values or ideology coming from within the party itself.

That is, at least not from within the national Labour Party. The localism of the New Politics has briefly flowered in Wales, where sensitivity to the socialist values of its electorate has allowed the Welsh Labour Party to make some electoral gains. In the 2003 local elections, when Labour was decimated nationally by the Conservatives, it made some advances in Wales. The Welsh party had adopted the abolition of prescription charges and other populist socialist ideas as the core of its own manifesto. As a result it won half the seats in the Welsh Assembly and even stole the Plaid Cymru heartlands of Islwyn and Rhondda. Where New Labour has devolved power and loosened its control, such as in Wales and London, the local parties have been shown capable of producing policies more sensitive to their local electorates than the front bench has privately urged them to be. If devolution were extended across the country then one might hypothesise that some local parties would produce policies to the right of New Labour, if they meet the priorities of its voters. This certainly has been the pattern of state government in America, where a male Republican governor in New York supports the right to abortion, but a female Democratic office holder in Arkansas opposes it.

But the national Labour Party remains a prisoner of the past. Policy changes brought about for electoral gain in the 1990s have eliminated the broader potential for dissent and have tied the party to the politics of the Third Way for the foreseeable future. Some commentators and many on the left within the Labour Party have argued that the presumed ascendancy of Gordon Brown to the leadership will mark the beginning of a sea change within British politics. It is true that the current dynamic between government and opposition that emerges from the personalities of their leaders will alter, but the evidence that Brown will signal a change of policy or philosophical direction is scant. His speech to the party's conference in 2005 gave overwhelming evidence for this. Although he provided the hall with a biographical explanation for his participation in government (Calvinistic morality and the importance of civic institutions) he took the opportunity to assure it that he was dedicated to the legacy of New Labour. This is hardly surprising. Brown was the architect of New Labour's economic programme, has con-sistently beefed up government spending on the war on terror and has publicly or at least theoretically endorsed its public-service reforms. His political future lies with courting the right of his party, not its already fairly devoted left. He needs to prevent the threat of a right-wing counter-candidacy and so will not move to antagonise Blairites within Parliament. Also in the age of triangulation what apparently attracts the grassroots of the union movement to Brown is an anathema to the prevailing political culture. Association with the left could prove Brown's Achilles heel and David Cameron has already moved cannily to portray the Chancellor as an obstacle to public-service reform, around which Tony Blair has constructed a new 'centre-ground'. For Brown not to accelerate or even endorse those reforms would open him up to charges of being 'Old' Labour. In sum, it will not benefit Brown to play to his party's left, reinvigorate socialism or even tentatively use the language of egalitarianism. He will move to the right. To quote the outgoing Prime Minister, 'It is sometimes said that Gordon is, you know, not New Labour, he is old Labour, he is a roadblock to reform. It is complete nonsense. He is completely and totally on the same lines as me.' His leadership will effect a change of style, a genuine familiarity with the trade unions, a new tone of homespun values and cautious pessimism. It is true that these things are very important to a Labour Party still withering under years of modernisation and being fashionable. But for the wider polity it will not mean significant change to the substance of debate and will not proffer relevant answers to Brown's own question of why we govern.

The impact of triangulation upon other parties and the shaping of British democracy are the concern of the following chapters, but two implications for government in the next few years can be dealt with directly here. The first is that Labour's entrapment in the past, particularly in the discourse of old versus new and the need to strike new ground between socialism and capitalism is, in some areas of policy, proving increasingly erroneous. The most potent example is in foreign policy. There is no simple 'Third Way' in foreign policy. This accounts for much of the confusion over policy between 1997 and 2001, when New Labour neglected to construct a coherent framework for its relations with the rest of the world. Thus it could both declare a new era of ethical foreign policy and complete an arms contract begun by the Major government with Robert Mugabe's Zimbabwe. Labour's intellectual focus upon the resolving of conflicts and debate rooted in the politics of the 1990s has in many areas prevented it from dedicating itself to the construction of an intellectual framework in relation to matters that do not refer to public services, macro-economics or industrial relations. In this context Brown's speech that wedded him to the New Labour project while avoiding all reference to military policy is understandable. There are some new questions to which the Third Way, consensus chasing and triangulation will not be equipped to provide effective answers.

The second, related, observation is that New Labour has carried out significant revisions and reforms of Britain, but has shied away from providing a clear vision of the future it hopes to build. It has altered the structure of the House of Lords, introduced devolution and set about addressing apparent failures in the legal system. Though many of these changes have been innovative, they have often flirted with revolution without embracing its natural conclusions. For instance, the scrapping of hereditary peers has left an unsatisfactory settlement in its wake. To many the obvious, ultimate end of democratisation is direct election of peers. Labour's preparedness to go half way is again typical of triangulation and evidence of its inability to solve some eternal questions. These innovations are not even representative of piecemeal reform, because they are not part of a natural progression towards a final utopian goal. This has been the root of some of the dissatisfaction felt with New Labour. It has avoided providing a new utopian narrative, or even an idea of national purpose. It does not talk about why it is in government, or even what it believes government can be used to do. The language of efficiency and good management, even if rooted in a generous public spirit, is not the natural way for parties of the left to engender and sustain support. Labour may declare itself a 'progressive' party, but it fails to clearly outline to what it intends to progress. If it plans to progress towards Alan Milburn's variety of aggressive collectivism, it may leave many liberals and left-wingers behind. Not only does this represent its break from the past, but it will also be a stimulus to growing sectors of the population seeking their political identity outside the mainstream political parties. This is the theme of this book's later chapters.

Despite all that this chapter has discussed, what remains the most remarkable characteristic of modern political debate is that, despite public and party disaffection with the government, New Labour remains one of the most successful post-war political movements. In her speech to the Fabians, Patricia Hewitt gave some indication of why this is. 'We cannot', she warned, 'rely upon our opposition remaining incompetent.' Tony Blair seems to have been sustained in government because his party's problems are symptomatic of a wider malaise in the British democratic system. He has been re-elected because the public did not feel they are currently being offered a viable alternative. He may stand accused of not offering a coherent vision for Britain, but the lack of a coherent opposition is perhaps significant of a wider crisis.

3

The Conservative Party

W. Somerset Maugham's book *The Razor's Edge* is the tale of a young American, Larry Darrell, in search of answers to questions he has not even asked. His spiritual quest, which embraces many lands and cultures, compels him to confront the many paths which are laid out before him. As he embarks on his intellectual journey, he in turn presents those around him with choices which reach into the very depths of their personalities. In Maugham's inimitable style, the tale proceeds neither as tragedy nor as comedy, without moral or purpose, and ultimately this epic story leaves us with nothing but the bare characters themselves. All but one are revealed as shallow, vain and self-obsessed. They are unlovable, unsatisfied and, crucially, unhappy. Only Larry, whose entire history has been forsaken and who appears to have lost the most, seems content.

The central dynamic of the book is provided by the contrast between Larry and his fiancée, Isobel. As Larry gradually begins to realise that there is something in him, something only half understood, that is driving him towards a life of reflection and contemplation, he starts to appreciate that the superficial life of wealth and frivolity that lies before him is inimical to the satisfaction of his gnawing desires. Although Isobel loves Larry dearly and initially has some sympathy with his emerging ideas, she is a young girl who wishes only to enjoy herself. She likes parties and dresses, dinners and dancing; she enjoys the shallow trappings of her station. Inevitably, she realises that she could not possibly live the life she loves with Larry and painfully breaks off their engagement to marry the son of a wealthy stockbroker. The key point is that each of them is confronted with the same choice and each of them is forced to live with the lasting consequences of their decision.

The book, which begins with a quotation from the Katha-Upanishad, ultimately proves the validity of its point: 'The sharp edge of a razor is difficult to pass over; thus the wise say the path to Salvation is hard.'

In the wake of the 2005 general election, the Conservative Party faced a choice comparable to the one which confronts Larry and Isobel in Maugham's book. It was clear that, more than ever before, a change was necessary. The Conservative Party had to become the viable alternative that Patricia Hewitt feared. They had to tackle the new political style pioneered by Tony Blair's Labour Party; they had to challenge the successful exercise of triangulation and spin. On the one hand, this could be achieved by recognising that New Labour's greatest strength was its mastery of the 'New Politics', which had fundamentally and irrevocably altered the nature of government and electioneering. The Conservatives could, in other words, become a 'newer' party than New Labour. They could be a more media-friendly party, a party which paid even more attention to focus groups, which anticipated the policy decisions of its opponents more effectively and which exploited the internal weaknesses of other parties with more damaging effects. On the other hand, however, the Conservative Party could become the 'viable alternative' by accepting that the New Politics was, in fact, Labour's greatest weakness. They could abandon the culture of spin, forget the policies of other parties and instead concentrate on developing a clear political identity of their own which could then be presented with conviction to the British electorate.

At the opening session of the Conservative Party conference in October 2005, the atmosphere amongst the delegates was electric. As Michael Howard prepared formally to resign, every person in the vast auditorium believed that the party was about to pass over the edge of its own razor. In the days that followed, the speeches by the five declared candidates for the leadership appeared to give some indication that the critical choice had already been made. The delegates' reaction to the speeches was important in this respect. Although still regarded as the front runner, with sixty-six MPs openly giving him their support, David Davis was criticised heavily for lacking personality, for being 'dull' and for putting substance over style. Liam Fox by contrast won more support than any analyst expected because of his flamboyant performance of an act which had little in the way of intellectual content or coherence. Ann Treneman, writing in the *Times*, suggested that he had ticked 'all the right boxes', but no commentator was able concisely to summarise his notion of 'Conservatism'. Meanwhile David Cameron, who ultimately carried the field, won much of his applause at the conference merely for his youthful appearance and 'modernising' reputation.

Watching the candidates' speeches as a casual observer from the back of the auditorium, it seemed as if the leadership election was being conducted on the basis purely of personality and presentation. As a component in the bigger choice facing the Conservative Party, it indicated that style, the handmaiden of spin, had already carried the field. Indeed, for many people, Kenneth Clarke's candidacy was emblematic of the election and of the determination of the party's future direction. Clarke, a former Chancellor of the Exchequer and Home Secretary, had unsuccessfully run for the leadership in 1997 and 2001 on a platform built around his beer-drinking, cigar-smoking, 'ordinary Joe' appearance and his reputation as a straight-talking political 'bruiser'. He lost on each of these occasions to candidates of far inferior experience as a result of his unfortunate association with governments of ill repute. The fact that he had decided to stand for a third time on exactly the same platform, however, reflected a belief that the party was in a position to consider his character and image sufficient grounds to elect him despite his membership of previous governments. Regardless of his fortunes at the hands of MPs and party members, the very possibility of his candidacy seemed predicated on a shift of attitudes towards general elections in favour of stylistic considerations, founded on a belief that the New Politics was not only here to stay but also there to be emulated.

For many commentators, Cameron's victory two months after the conference was a confirmation of this trend. Cameron, an Eton- and Oxford-educated 39-year-old with only four years' experience as an MP, had begun the race as a rank outsider with little name recognition outside of the House of Commons. His charming style and boyish appearance, along with his skilful media management and avoidance of controversy during the campaign, led not only ultimately to success but, more importantly, also to comparisons with Blair. His victory speech on 6 December 2005 seemed to give credence to this evaluation. Whereas William Hague, Iain Duncan Smith and Michael Howard had each used their victory speeches to give a clear indication of the direction in which they intended to take the party, Cameron spoke primarily in terms of image and behaviour. 'We will change the way we look,' he said, and added, 'we need to change the way we feel.' The old image of the Conservative Party as a collection of backwards-looking, middle-class white men would, he suggested, be the first thing to be changed, thus illustrating the significance of appearance and popular appeal to his approach. Equally, he spoke neither of policy initiatives nor of guiding principles, but rather of the 'challenges' facing Britain. Change and action were emphasised frequently but the character of this change and the nature of this action were barely touched upon. The appearance of alteration and the image of revision seemed to be more important to the new leader than the direction of change itself.

The ascendancy of style, however, was delusory. Although the high-profile campaign launches and photo-calls of the late autumn indicated that Conservative MPs and activists were searching for a 'media-friendly' candidate to lead them to victory in the next election, this was more a consequence of the party's decision on its electoral system than a result of any confidence in the New Politics as a means of conducting government.

Shortly after announcing his intention to resign in the aftermath of the election, Howard put forward proposals to limit the franchise in leadership elections to Conservative MPs. For a number of months it seemed possible that the party would accept these proposals and likely that, even if they were rejected, a greater say would be given to members of Parliament than to rank-and-file activists. During this period many of the figures who later emerged as key players in the leadership contest gave speeches to think-tanks and political societies in which they considered the very meaning of the word 'Conservative' in great detail. The approach in almost all was philosophical and the manner was considered and thoughtful. It was not that the question of leadership was immaterial in this period. Rather, it was seen as merely a small component in a much bigger picture. Barely a month after the general election, David Willetts, then shadow Secretary of State for Trade and Industry, told the Social Market Foundation:

> If the next Conservative leader turns out to be the most charismatic politician since Lloyd George, if they preside over an organisation more efficient than Tesco's, we still won't win the next election unless we can answer two fundamental questions: 'What does Conservatism stand for in the Britain of the twenty-first century?' and 'Why should many more people than today feel the need to have a Conservative government instead of the alternative?'

The problem, Willetts suggested, was not who would lead the Conservative Party but what that Conservative Party would represent. The party's disappointment at the 2005 general election was not a consequence of Howard's leadership style, but a result of the party's platform. In an article in the *Daily Telegraph*, Bernard Jenkin, the shadow minister for energy, argued that 'the reason we were beaten again is voters still think we are just in it for ourselves rather than for a higher principle. The question on which we must agree is: what is that principle?'

Once it had been decided that it would be the ordinary party members and not MPs who would have the final say in the leadership election, however, the question of principle appeared to have been forgotten both by the media and by the candidates. The candidates – whittled down, by this stage, from a potential nine to a likely five[1] – stopped discussing differences of principle and, with the exception of David Davis, instead concentrated on emphasising their appearance in an attempt to win the support of an electorate composed of activists and not merely colleagues. Yet while this certainly occurred, it would be a mistake to assume that the discussion of Conservative principle simultaneously became an unimportant factor in the determination of the party's political future and electoral prospects. The rarefied debate of the summer months had not been forgotten; the strong opinions held by senior figures were not revoked; and the intense divisions that had been created had not healed, despite the appearance of shifting loyalties. Pure common sense, however, dictated that a bitter election campaign fought on the basis of different interpretations of the same political creed would cause very public rifts in the wider party at a sensitive time. From the perspective of party unity and from that of individual candidates, it was therefore expedient to postpone the debate until well after the new leader had been decided.

Once Cameron had acceded to the leadership, the electoral need to preserve the appearance of unity was translated into a party-political need to involve the various factions in the formation of a new shadow Cabinet and a new direction. Although Cameron had been elected with a large majority (133,446 votes to Davis's 64,398), it was necessary for him to proceed with caution with respect to his parliamentary colleagues. The new leader could not at the moment of his victory launch into a detailed explanation of policy objectives or deliver a powerful statement of his guiding principles. Such an action would have risked alienating those MPs and activists whose preference earlier in the leadership election might have been for a candidate with a radically different conception of 'Conservatism'. Rather than risking conflict, it was necessary for Cameron to begin tackling the different party factions by attempting to build a broad-based consensus. Hence in his victory speech he sensibly focused on challenges and drew attention to the need for a period of reflection, which, no doubt, would involve consultation and consideration well away from the public eye. The divisions of the early summer of 2005, which had for so many months been painstakingly concealed, had to be addressed in preparation for the next general election, but addressed carefully and discreetly. The appearance of a devotion to style was therefore a necessary public screen for a private and long-overdue debate.

Far from following the superficial path of Somerset Maugham's Isobel, the Conservative Party had apparently decided well before the conference to pursue Larry's path of considered reflection. However, it still remains to be seen whether this path will indeed ultimately lead them to Salvation. To explain this, and to understand the Conservatives' reaction to the New Politics of triangulation and spin, it is important to look at the critical battle over 'Conservatism' that was left behind during the later stages of the leadership election.

The problem of 'Conservatism'

Michael Howard led the Conservative Party into the 2005 general election with a campaign based on six simple pledges: more police, cleaner hospitals, lower taxes, school discipline, controlled immigration, accountability. The messages were clear and forceful, but they singularly failed to win significant support and, once the election was over, they were quickly repudiated by Tory politicians. For many MPs, the pledges represented the wrong sort of Conservative Party. Yet if the six pledges were wrong, what did it mean to be a Conservative?

Conservatism itself is the most difficult branch of British politics to summarise effectively. Unlike Labour, the Conservative Party has no historical ties to a single set of well-defined principles and is bound to no established creed. Historically speaking, it is a phantasm, a cloud of mist that appears to have form but defies anyone wishing to get a firm hold. Since its inception, it has had no concrete ideological identity and no definitive statement of purpose.

Broadly speaking, those who describe themselves as Conservatives are contemptuous of political theory. They see themselves as practical people, as pragmatists and have little or no time for idealism or philosophising. If they are united by anything, it is by what Edmund Burke described in 1770 as 'a common principle that is in the national interest'. When they describe themselves as 'Conservatives' they use the term in what Benjamin Disraeli called 'its purest and loftiest sense', to mean a pride in 'belonging to a great country', to express a 'wish to maintain its greatness' and to reflect their belief that '[this] greatness [should be] attributed to the ancient institutions of the land'.

This emphasis on the nation and its prosperity may be the essence of Conservatism, but most of those who espouse it would agree that it does not amount to anything approaching a coherent political philosophy. It is a vague belief, a collection of strong emotions coupled with a barely justified faith in the historical value of British institutions, but it is not sufficient material from which to construct a detailed theory of politics as the basis for legislative action. The crucial element that is missing is a clear definition of what the 'national interest' actually represents. Whereas the Labour Party has traditionally derived its conception of the common profit from a preconceived notion of human nature, the Conservative Party has no such ontological basis.

Nevertheless, in seeking to govern a country, it is necessary even for the most practical, anti-ideological party to have some model of the national interest, if only for the sake of providing a solid foundation for a coherent set of policies. In the case of the Conservative Party, pragmatism and preference have served in place of ontology. Successive leaders in the modern era conceived a particular notion of what was most critical for the good of the United Kingdom. This led to often radically different manifestos being offered at consecutive elections.

Generally, however, the Conservative Party has oscillated between two different interpretations of the 'national interest'. The first is the liberal-economic interpretation. This view holds that the nation's prosperity should be conceived in essentially economic terms and is best advanced through a minimum of government intervention. Individual British people are generally held to be hard-working, industrious characters who not only deserve to be free from external intervention but when left alone can also deliver the greatest benefit to the entire country.

In many senses, this interpretation of Conservatism is greatly indebted to the work of Adam Smith. In *The Wealth of Nations*, Smith strongly opposed the belief that governments were best placed to manage affairs which touched individuals most particularly:

> All systems either of preference or of restraint, therefore, being thus completely taken away, the obvious and simple system of natural liberty establishes itself of its own accord. Every man, as long as he does not violate the laws of justice, is left perfectly free to pursue his own interest his own way, and to bring both his industry and capital into competition with those of any other man or order of men. The sovereign [politician] is completely discharged from a duty, in the attempting to perform which he must always be exposed to innumerable delusions, and for the proper performance of which no human wisdom or knowledge could ever be sufficient: the duty of superintending the industry of private people.

This faith in people's capacity to determine the best course of

national affairs naturally goes hand in hand with a belief in the validity
of people's ability to deliver economic benefits by pursuing their own
individual interests. As Smith put it:

> Every individual necessarily labours to render the annual revenue of the society
> as great as he can. He generally indeed neither intends to promote the public
> interest, nor knows how much he is promoting it. He intends only his own gain,
> and he is in this, as in many other cases, led by an invisible hand to promote an
> end which was no part of his intention. By pursuing his own interest he
> frequently promotes that of the society more effectually than when he really
> intends to promote it. I have never known much good done by those who
> affected to trade for the public good.

These texts could be seen as commandments for the liberal–economic
interpretation of Conservatism.

The second interpretation is the socially paternalistic view of the
government's relationship with the people of Britain. Many historians
have seen the strength of this interpretation of Conservatism as lying in
its aristocratic roots. Although this is a somewhat uncharitable and
misleading representation, there is some merit in the description. Those
who in the 1960s and 1970s espoused this interpretation of their
political creed included only a few nobles in their number but they
were bound together by what could be described as a rather aristocratic
sense of duty to their country. Inordinately proud of their nation, they
believed that it was their responsibility not only to perpetuate Britain's
'greatness' in foreign affairs but also to do their utmost to help and
defend the less fortunate and the needy. It was in every sense a socially
paternalistic interpretation, marked by a willingness to intervene in
economic affairs to ensure that no one was left behind or left wanting,
and characterised by a strong desire not to take any risks when managing
the economy.

These two interpretations contain elements which are obviously
contradictions, despite the fact that they are each derived from the same
essential conception of Conservatism. To counter this inescapable fact,
the Conservative Party has conventionally employed pragmatic restraint
to prevent troublesome inconsistencies from appearing in a particular

programme. To take an example, Edward Heath was a Prime Minister who was attached to a broadly paternalistic interpretation of the political creed, yet he was careful also to accept that there were limits to its application. Given the problems in Britain during his premiership, he was careful not to advocate the extension of social paternalism to include the unrestricted support of nationalised industries or the pursuit of a weak policy towards the unreasonable demands of trade unions. Without causing inconsistencies in his programme, Heath restrained the logical extension of his paternalistic impulses in line with what on the one hand was nationally desirable and on the other hand was feasible. Similarly, although John Major may well have pursued many of the features of Thatcherite economic liberalism, he nevertheless recognised that growing social problems required the continuing involvement of the state in certain key areas of domestic policy. The logical extremes of the liberal-economic interpretation were restrained by a pragmatic assessment of the situation. To summarise briefly, prag-matism has usually meant that liberal economics has been moderated by social consideration, and social paternalism has been tempered by the recognition of the economic benefits of some degree of liberalisation. Despite the contradictions between social paternalism and economic liberalism, manifestos and policy programmes had until 1997 always been carefully managed to find some measure of common ground and thereby preserve coherence.

The wilderness years: the failure of Conservative triangulation and the rise of factional discontent

For many years after its devastating defeat at the 1997 general election, the Conservative Party was placed in a quandary. Labour's reinvention, its skilful management of the media and its effective triangulation of policy placed the remaining Tory MPs in a very difficult and confusing position. The traditional debate between liberal-economic and socially paternalistic interpretations of Conservatism suddenly seemed to have been eclipsed by the advent of a new Labour Party which was both capable of and willing to hijack the best elements of each branch of thought, propounding right-wing liberal policies just as readily as it deployed communitarian arguments. The Conservatives, led by the personally brilliant but untested William Hague, suddenly lost confidence in their familiar attitude of finding common ground between the two interpretations of their political creed as the basis for political action. They became obsessed with 'getting ahead of the game', with generating policies along New Labour lines before members of the Cabinet could announce them. Image, tactical selection of policy and media management were the order of the day. Dozens of documents were produced which unsuccessfully attempted to emulate Labour's triangulation policy and the 2001 manifesto appeared as little more than an effort to out-New Labour the Labour Party, while giving some reassurance to the Conservative old guard.

Without becoming any less Conservative in their personal beliefs, members of the parliamentary party had lost sight of the internal debate between liberal economics and social paternalism. Instead, they devoted themselves to pursuing the strategic approach, which, it was believed, had brought Tony Blair such staggering success. The two opposing interpretations of Conservatism did not disappear: rather, they willingly entertained the idea that their battle with each other for the heart of the party was less significant than the party's strategic battle with Labour.

After the 2001 election, however, the situation began to alter somewhat. There is no doubt that the party's dismal performance at the polls had something to do with this. Gaining only one seat after four years in opposition appeared a poor return for the effort that had been put into emulating New Labour. It became apparent that the attempts to reproduce Alastair Campbell's media success and the government's popularity at the polls had failed dismally. In those dark weeks after the election, many MPs thought back miserably to the embarrassing occasion of Hague's visit to a theme park wearing a baseball hat in a bid to appear 'in touch' and 'down to earth'. The episode, which had made politicians, journalists and voters wince even at the time, seemed to Conservative MPs to encapsulate the failures of the past four years.

Under the carefully managed surface discontent began to grow. The party's public profile dropped significantly and public faith in the Conservatives as a potential government all but evaporated. Despite some limited success in parliamentary debates, the wider strategic battle with Labour was fought and lost many times. By the middle of July 2001, the Conservatives had dropped to a depressing low of 25 per cent in the opinion polls and Labour were enjoying a record 27-point lead. The media presented the Conservative Party as a ship without a rudder, battered by the winds on a dangerous sea. Outside the party itself, the strategy of triangulation pursued so successfully by New Labour began to generate dissatisfaction in the country at large. Labour was perceived as a party which lacked any real substance, which was attached only to the retention of power, and which was dominated by 'spin' and style. Observing these developments, Conservative MPs believed there was only one conclusion to draw: the strategic battle was leading nowhere. The attempt to 'get ahead of the game' was failing miserably, the tactics employed were becoming increasingly unpopular with the electorate and the party itself was suffering as a result of its emulation of Labour. No matter how unpopular the government became, as long as the Conservatives tried to model themselves on New Labour, Labour would always emerge triumphant. A growing number of Tory MPs argued that what was needed to combat New Labour was not a more effective form of triangulation but a stronger attachment to a definite set of principles and the establishment of a credible political philosophy that could be sold to the electorate with confidence and conviction.

The two interpretations of Conservatism reared their heads once again, but they did so quietly. Having been damaged so significantly by accusations of disunity in the past, the party was anxious not to risk sliding any further in the polls. Under Iain Duncan Smith, who ominously assumed the leadership on 11 September 2001, the Conservatives maintained a façade of continuity, publicly changing their position very little while behind the scenes discussion continued with growing fervour. Despite the fact that the strategy of triangulation had been discredited, a belief prevailed that any arguments over Conservative principles and the direction of the party should be conducted behind closed doors and, so far as was possible, in secrecy. The party's public image was regarded as paramount and no different strategy or platform was to be announced before the debate had run its course. This desire to preserve a veneer of peace and unity was intense.

Although in one sense this was wise, it stifled real discussion and a genuine reconsideration of the party's direction. It was, perhaps, a paranoid reaction to what was, in reality, the ideal time for just such a debate.

In the summer of 2003, I was asked to make a television programme with the BBC to coincide with the party conference. The idea was that in the course of a half-hour show I would comment on the debates at the conference. Naturally, during preparation I gave the producer a preliminary impression of my attitude towards the party's programme. My views were quite forceful and drew strongly on the essence of the differences between the two interpretations of Conservatism. The BBC, quite properly, asked the leadership to comment on what I had said. Two days before the first of the filming was to begin in Cambridge, I received a telephone call relaying a message from the leader's office. I had been expelled. Three months later, long after the conference, I was reinstated without application or explanation.

My expulsion and subsequent reinstatement illustrates the extreme paranoia which surrounded the initial re-emergence of debate within the Conservative Party. Many senior party figures were of the opinion that the arguments which were central to the revival of the party were being suppressed because of an unnecessarily extreme desire to preserve a show of public unity. Change of whatever kind, it was felt, was coming too slowly. MORI polls showed that the public was more dissatisfied with the Labour government than at any time since its election in 1997. Half of all British voters thought that Tony Blair should resign as Prime Minister. The Conservative Party needed to stop trying to make itself another New Labour and to take advantage of a positive change in the political mood with a new approach. By the late autumn of 2003, the sense of frustration reached fever pitch and Duncan Smith was brutally ousted on an insignificant premise.

Under Michael Howard debate gathered pace, but with a general election looming, disagreement was still constrained. Throughout 2004, speeches were given and pamphlets published by senior members of the party which clearly reflected the resurgence of discussion. Just beneath the public façade, it was perfectly obvious that the Conservative Party was embroiled in one of the most animated and extreme arguments over its specific political orientation in recent history. The imminence of the election, however, meant that the growing excitement surrounding the debate was inevitably muffled and, under the careful management of the joint chairmen of the party, Lord Saatchi and Liam Fox, the intense arguments were largely concealed from public view. If the demise of Duncan Smith had signalled the end of Conservative triangulation and the renaissance of the age-old tradition of liberal-economic versus socially paternalistic debate, the anticipated election demanded an inevitable restraint to the public manifestation of the arguments. As 2005 began, therefore, Howard assumed the appearance of a young racing driver who had finally opened the throttle on his vehicle and was desperately struggling to apply the brakes before approaching the first corner of a critical race.

Howard's six election pledges were incontestably Conservative. The undertaking to provide more police, to control immigration and to uphold the accountability of Parliament were perfectly in keeping with the party's traditional belief in preserving the integrity of British institutions and the security and wellbeing of the population as a whole. In a similar fashion, the focus on restrained government intervention in economic affairs reflected in the promise of lower taxes was commensurate with the party's familiar links with Smithian liberalism, whilst the pledge to deliver cleaner hospitals and improved school discipline was a manifestation of the party's social paternalism working broadly within the framework of state-provided services.

Yet for all the 2005 manifesto's impeccably Conservative credentials, it was a document which caused considerable dissent within the party. Although few had specific problems with the desire to improve policing, monitor immigration more closely and strengthen the accountability of Parliament, many MPs perceived great tension between the economic liberalism of lower taxation and the social paternalism that lay behind the document's social elements.

In explaining the party's economic policy, the manifesto stated: 'We will lower taxes. We believe that people should choose how their money is spent . . . Lower taxes promote enterprise and growth. But they also promote the right values.' This implied not only a faith in the operation of Adam Smith's 'invisible hand', but also seemed to express a confidence in the value of a broader liberalisation. If people are believed to be better able than any government to decide how to spend their money for their own benefit and for the greater national good, then it follows that the market could better provide for their care, support and education than centrally managed organisations. Detailing the party's approach to healthcare, the manifesto stated:

> Choice gives people power, a sense of purpose and control. It makes those who offer a service accountable to those who use it. It will give patients the clean hospitals and the shorter waiting times they want. Our policies will give everyone the kind of choice in healthcare that today only money can buy.

This initially appears to extend the implications of economic liberalism into the sphere of social services. Yet, where one might have expected to see some kind of a promise to open up the NHS to private healthcare companies, there was nothing: only a pledge to give patients and GPs 'the right to choose the hospital or carer that is right for them'. While an effort had been made to repeat the earlier faith in the operation of the 'invisible hand', it proved to be no more than a gesture. A paternalistic desire to provide healthcare for all through a national health service was maintained. Similarly, while choice was promised in education, the commitment to the market was not matched by a willingness to open the school system up to private companies.

The 2005 Conservative manifesto respected elements of both interpretations of the party's core beliefs in a way which did deliver a measure of coherence. It was, in many senses, an attempt to cherry-pick the best aspects of the two different interpretations while avoiding the worst effects of the growing conflict within the party. In the climate of heated debate, it was a document of compromise. The fact that so many Conservative members of Parliament disparaged it as a confused text and condemned the tension they perceived was not therefore a consequence of anything specific in the manifesto itself, but rather a result of the fact that the party had divided itself into very different factions long before the election itself had occurred. Tired of being beaten by the extraordinary success of Labour's triangulation policy, the body of the parliamentary party had decided that it was time not to continue the emulation of such a strategy but to determine a distinct and clear identity for the party.

Despite the media's attempt to present the party as being divided between 'traditionalists' (led by David Davis) and 'modernisers' (led by David Cameron), the fault-lines of debate were in origin precisely the same as they had been for several decades. On the one hand, there were those who propounded a liberal-economic interpretation of Conservatism. Known as the 'Soho' modernisers, this group was represented most cogently by Davis, Cameron and Bernard Jenkin. On the other hand, there were those who favoured a socially paternalistic approach. Dubbed the 'Easterhouse' modernisers, this group was championed by David Willetts, Iain Duncan Smith, Oliver Letwin and Theresa May. The foundations of each faction were derived directly from the two historical interpretations of Conservative thought. The problem lay in the fact that, having been constrained and frustrated by the unsuccessful pursuit of a Conservative triangulation strategy, each faction had pushed its premises to logical conclusions more radical and more extreme than ever before. Frustration had fuelled the generation of two highly immoderate and even revolutionary forms of Conservatism.

The Soho modernisers

It was Iain Duncan Smith who first brought the sobriquets 'Soho' and 'Easterhouse' to public attention, in an article in the *Times* on 22 May 2005. Although his purpose was to defend the latter faction as the best hope both for the Conservative Party and for Britain's future, he incidentally provided an extremely succinct definition of the rival faction. The Soho modernisers, he wrote, 'want a more permissive and liberal Conservatism'. They drew their heritage directly from that element of Conservative belief which owed the most to Adam Smith, but they had gone further than any previous Tory thinkers. For this section of the party, it was self-evident that freedom was a good in itself. Bernard Jenkin, in a speech to the Policy Exchange think-tank, revisited Burke's definition of the party and concluded that his '"common principle" for the Conservative Party at the start of the twenty-first century must address freedom, democracy and our position in the world'. 'People', he stated, 'want more freedom, not more government.'

This freedom was essentially an economic form of freedom, but at the same time, it was an implicit faith in the absolute validity of Smith's 'invisible hand' that prompted it to become the basis for thought on all other areas of policy. This was perhaps expressed most clearly in a speech David Davis gave to the Centre for Policy Studies in July 2005. In this speech, Davis detailed the reasons for an economic policy which was dominated by less regulation of industry and a preoccupation with the absolute good of lower taxation. Yet, he said:

> Our economic policy must not appear as if it exists for its own sake – a proper subject for Budget Day and the *FT*. It must appear as what it is – the engine for a better life for all. The fact is that only a low-tax, light-regulation economy can provide the resources for good healthcare and education, roads and police. But more than that, a growing economy is the only way to provide wider opportunity for all. It is the only way to provide pensions which keep or increase their value. It is the only way to allow people to save, and so to acquire property without falling deeper into debt. It is the only sustainable way of creating jobs and so lifting people out of poverty. In the same fashion, we Tories have to make the case that reforming the welfare system isn't principally a question of cash resources, but of human resources – of building character and motivation, so everyone who is able to participate constructively and gainfully in society can do so.[2]

The equation Davis was proposing was simple: economic freedom created the conditions for social improvement without government intervention. The market, left to its own devices, would provide. Individuals, if left alone, would bring the whole nation rewards. The manner in which he put it, including his interesting reference to 'human resources', however, made it clear that Davis perceived the ideas behind the 'invisible hand' to be applicable well beyond the confines of economic policy, the limits of taxation and regulation. This theme was taken up and extended by Davis's leadership rival, David Cameron. Davis and Cameron were erroneously presented as being from opposite ends of the Conservative spectrum but, as their speeches demonstrate, their approaches were virtually identical in all respects apart from presentation. Substantially, Davis's 'traditionalism' and Cameron's 'modernism' were impossible to separate. On this occasion, Cameron extended Davis's belief in the beneficial effects of unrestrained market forces to argue for the abolition of the 'apartheid . . . between public and private' in all areas of the public sector. As well as opening up healthcare to private competition, education would be revised to allow for the operation of similar market forces. Ruth Lea, the director of the Centre for Policy Studies, has suggested that 'the way forward for [both] education and health is to get the state out of the provision of these services'. As Davis put it, 'the natural forces of competition would drive up standards. And we would bring to an end the perverse consequence of State monopoly which has been to the benefit of the better off and the strong at the expense of the poorest and the weak.'[3]

Unafraid of stopping in his pursuit of freedom at the reform of the NHS and the Department for Education and Skills, Cameron proposed the establishment of 'police authorities with directly elected police commissioners' as a means of making 'the police more locally accountable in a way they simply have not been before'. Similarly, Jenkin argued that the Conservative Party should 'give back real freedom and power to local communities to control their own affairs. In England, this means nothing less than the restoration of genuine shire and city self-government.'[4] For Sir Malcolm Rifkind, the shadow Work and Pensions Secretary, who later tried to present himself as a 'one nation' Conservative, it was essential to 'return local power to local communities' in such a way that 'includes greater control over the service that local people use'.[5] Using the market as their model, the Soho modernisers argued not only that freedom was a good in itself, but that greater liberty delivered better services in all areas. It was, therefore, almost heretical for them to accept willingly the restrictions placed on their liberal agenda in the 2005 election manifesto.

The attachment to economic freedom initially makes the Soho modernisers appear as the spiritual heirs of Margaret Thatcher. Yet their guiding principles of freedom and choice in all areas of domestic policy make it difficult simply to classify them as unreconstructed Thatcherites.

They are, if anything, a stripped-down, theory-light manifestation of Thatcher's legacy. On account of the independence of the Bank of England, they are unencumbered by a sophisticated approach to economic theory and have been left to expand the implications of economic liberalism far further than even she imagined. If anything, they bear a greater theoretical similarity to that form of Liberalism which reached its zenith under W. E. Gladstone. In modern times, however, the Soho modernisers are perhaps best compared to the American Republican Party. Although the Republicans would likely baulk at being described as liberal, it is with this branch of thought that they share much of their political philosophy. Like the Soho modernisers, the Republicans generally judge that central government should be responsible only for those most critical functions which cannot be performed at a more devolved level, such as defence and foreign policy, and adhere to the belief that the best government is that which governs least. Having observed the success of the centre-right in American Congressional politics since 1994, and witnessed the impressive results achieved by a widespread domestic economic liberalism, there would be some cause for those in this faction of the Conservative Party to gain confidence in the validity of their programme for Britain's future.

The Easterhouse modernisers

The Easterhouse modernisers are strongly critical of the approach of their Soho rivals. David Willetts, in his speech to the Social Market Foundation, delivered a strong rebuke and at the same time underlined the reasons for his own attitudes:

> There are some serious problems with [the Soho modernisers'] strategy. It is no accident that it has become associated with the triviality of how we look. It risks becoming a bit like a *Fast Show* sketch – an obsession with 'does my bum look big in this?' politics. This is because deep down it is all about me, the individual. It is about expanding the sphere in which individuals can freely express themselves. But the Conservative Party's problem is not getting more about the individual, 'me', into its philosophy. We have already been saying this loud and

clear. The challenge is to explain where 'other people' fit in. It is the other people who change an individual life into a meaningful part of the family, a neighbourhood, or a nation.

Noticing the similarity between the Soho modernisers and the Republican Party, Willetts went on to explain how the apparent success of the latter was delusory and pointed out that even the most senior members of that party had recognised the need to address the collective as much as the individual:

> We sometimes talk as if government is like the thick snow on Alpine meadows: as it melts away a thousand flowers bloom just by forces of nature. But government disengagement doesn't automatically solve our social problems. . . . In his 2000 campaign, Bush attacked 'the destructive mindset: the idea that if Government would only get out of the way, all our problems would be solved. An approach with no higher goal, no nobler purpose, than "leave us alone".' We talk as if the problem is just the supply of government. . . . I believe the real problem has been the demand for government that grows as a consequence of a fractured and fragmented society. . . . Atomised individuals need more external support.

Willetts' speech neatly encapsulated the central tenets of the Easterhouse modernisers' approach. Rather than beginning from an absolute faith in the operation of economic liberalism and the 'invisible hand', they began from a deeply felt conviction that there were very real social problems in Britain that could only be solved by concerted government effort. This is communicated in the very name 'Easterhouse'. Visiting the Easterhouse estate in Glasgow in February 2002, Iain Duncan Smith (then leader of the party) was horrified at the extent and severity of inner-city deprivation. In a speech to the Conservative spring conference only weeks later, he spoke of the visit almost as an epiphany and unequivocally declared what he believed to be the vital need for the state to act to improve the lives of people like those he had met in Easterhouse. The consciously self-applied name 'Easterhouse' was therefore a deliberate indication of the concerns most important to its adherents.

Easterhouse Conservatism has as its rallying cry not 'freedom', but 'social justice'. Those who associate themselves with its principles believe that politics should have a definite moral purpose, that a political party should reach out to actively help the poor, the dispossessed and the needy rather than entrusting their fate entirely to the uncertain operations of a market composed of 'atomised individuals'. They hold, for example, that it is often the less well off and those who live alone who make most use of the accident and emergency wards of hospitals, not because they suffer from more serious injuries but because they have no other source of help to turn to. It is the government's job, Easterhouse modernisers believe, to support such people with a reliable, well-functioning health service. In turn, they suggest that while it is necessary to deal harshly with criminal offences involving drugs, greater effort should be put into encouraging schemes which attempt to deal with the causes of drug use, particularly in deprived areas.

In economic policy, although the Easterhouse modernisers do recognise the potential benefits of low taxation, they do not regard it as an end in itself. For them, the point is to recognise that tax cuts should be part of a much broader programme which respects the practicality of such measures as well as the need to provide a high standard of public services. They have in this way come to question whether tax cuts would be feasible or even desirable. The emphasis on centrally directed social justice naturally leads them to respect the need for a high level of public spending and hence they argue that there may actually be little room for lowering taxation. The option of opening up public services to private providers is met with scepticism. It may be a good thing, they have contended, but it might not actually reduce the cost of those services and thereby allow for tax cutbacks. In this sense, the Easterhouse modernisers have come to set less store by the value of lower taxation and the worth of greater private involvement in the public sector.

It is not so much that the Easterhouse modernisers regard the issue of 'freedom' as unimportant, but rather that they believe it to be overstated in comparison with the moral obligation of government to support the weakest members of society. Their approach is to an extent more paternalistic and more actively compassionate. They are the heirs of the 'aristocratic' social paternalism of the past, the spiritual successors of Harold Macmillan, but they have pushed it to the point where they seem almost to share similarities with those noble reformers of the nineteenth century who had links with Christian socialism and with the arguments of the liberation theologians of the 1980s and 1990s.

'Resolution': appeasement, attrition and triangulation

The difficulty of reconciling the two factions of the Conservative Party need not be laboured. Whereas the Soho modernisers' beliefs lead them towards a programme comprising an absolute commitment to lower taxation, industrial deregulation, the total restructuring of public services and the greater devolution of authority, the Easterhouse modernisers have tied themselves to policies which include increasing funding to 'community-based poverty-fighting organisations', the reform of the welfare state to give greater support to children, pensioners and the disabled, measures to promote 'family and community life' and allowing for tax reduction only where the burden of public spending allows. Each considered as a whole, the two approaches to the reform of the Conservative Party are almost completely incompatible and this was reflected in the vitriolic exchanges that took place between senior members of the party in late summer 2005. Alan Duncan, the shadow transport secretary, bitterly described the 'socially conservative' wing of the party as the 'Tory Taliban'. Similarly, Edward Leigh MP, in defending the foundation of the traditionally right-wing and morally conservative Cornerstone Group, argued that the Soho approach, with its dedication to liberal economics, was excessively 'managerial' and criticised them for lacking 'vision'.

In any policy-related debate in politics, however, there has to be a resolution and this was readily acknowledged by senior party members even before the result of the final ballot was known. Shortly after he was elected to the leadership, David Cameron appointed a shadow Cabinet which seemed to be reflective of a desire to reunite a party which was still subtly fragmented. MPs of every intellectual complexion were included in the mix and the overall impression was of a shadow Cabinet which had been constructed not only to appease the two factions but also as a prelude to the development of consensus. While Cameron quite naturally appointed those with whom he had the closest political affinity to key posts, he took care to invest senior Easterhouse Conservatives with important briefs. Hence, while George Osborne was confirmed as shadow Chancellor and Alan Duncan was made shadow Secretary of State for Trade and Industry, David Willetts was given responsibility for education, Theresa May was made shadow Leader of the Commons and Iain Duncan Smith was charged with developing policy on social justice. This apparent move towards compromise seems to be reflected in Cameron's identification of the six key challenges facing Britain. While issues of central importance to Soho Conservatives – such as economic competitiveness and national security – were highlighted strongly, the new leader was also careful to draw attention to concerns of greater importance to Easterhouse modernisers, such as social justice and the improvement of public services.

Despite this implicit stress on unity and consensus, however, there remains the fact that Cameron's Soho Conservatism is, even with his fondness for 'compassion', philosophically incompatible with the social paternalism of the Easterhouse modernisers. The leader's most cherished beliefs, such as in the remedial effects of economic liberalisation, remain at odds with the principles which have been espoused for so long by senior members of his shadow Cabinet and even by his new director of policy and research, Oliver Letwin. Regardless of his skilful management of people, Cameron had, by the beginning of 2006, given no evidence of any serious attempt to reconcile the two branches of thought.

It is tempting to suggest that Cameron was unwilling to instigate such an open process of reconciliation. As has already been stated, the contradictions of Soho and Easterhouse Conservatism are sufficiently stark that an open debate would have been even more unpleasant than what actually occurred in the late summer of 2005. Rather, his approach was designed to achieve the dominance of Soho Conservatism through the façade of compromise. This approach had three distinct components: appeasement, attrition and triangulation.

In the first place, Cameron set about giving the impression that each of the two branches of Conservative thought could be given primacy in different policy areas. While the Soho modernisers Osborne, Duncan and David Davis were given sway over the treasury, trade and home affairs respectively, Easterhouse modernisers appeared to be handed control of key aspects of social policy, reflected in Willett's appointment to the education brief and Duncan Smith's much vaunted task of rethinking the party's approach to social justice. Yet even though the Easterhouse modernisers were apparently satisfied by these appointments, the terms of the party's announcements on social policy demonstrated that this strategy was little more than appeasement. Lip service alone was paid to the social paternalism of Easterhouse Conservatism. A good illustration of this may be found in the 'beliefs' published shortly after Cameron's accession. The document stated:

> We believe in personal responsibility. But not in selfish individualism. So let us tackle the challenge of an increasingly atomised society by showing that personal responsibility is part of a shared responsibility; that we're all in this together; that there's a 'we' in politics as well as a 'me'.[6]

The language was unmistakably evocative of Willetts's powerful speech to the Social Market Foundation in June 2005 and appears to indicate a genuine willingness to adopt the social concern of the Easterhouse modernisers. Yet, while the document openly declares a belief in 'society', it simultaneously denies that the state has any responsibility to directly address social problems and restricts the function of government to that of a facilitator. 'Civic society' is to be helped to solve its own problems through charitable and voluntary organisations. By the same token, although the pressing need to reform healthcare and the provision of education was acknowledged, improvements were to be delivered 'without burdening today's generations with higher taxes, or tomorrow's generations with higher debt'. The centralised organisation of a well-funded series of public services advocated by Easterhouse modernisers was here sacrificed to an absolute commitment to lowering taxation and increasing 'choice, competition and local autonomy'.

The appeasement of the Easterhouse modernisers – vital to the establishment of party unity – therefore allowed Cameron to use the language of paternalism with respect to social issues, while simultaneously undercutting the principles upon which that branch of Conservatism was based. This gradual attrition of social paternalism was facilitated not only by the tremendous advantage of the leadership but also by the most significant intellectual weakness of Easterhouse Conservatism. The Easterhouse modernisers are moralists: their approach begins from a deep-seated sense of justice and right; they see ends first and means second. Although figures such as Willetts remain sceptical about the capacity of liberal economic principles to protect the most vulnerable members of society, this scepticism is only very vague and extremely ill stated. If the Easterhouse modernisers had ground to cede, therefore, it was with respect to their uncertainty over means. Given that, upon becoming leader, Cameron restated his absolute commitment to lower taxation and private involvement in healthcare, it was possible for him forcefully to suggest that the social concerns of the Easterhouse modernisers could best be satisfied by liberal economic means. Having gained the advantage with the desirability of private involvement in the public sector and the commensurate commitment to lower taxation, however, it was only natural for Cameron to have objected to more interventionist domestic poverty-fighting schemes by arguing against any substantial increases in public spending. While the terminology of the Easterhouse modernisers was preserved and key proponents of its version of Conservatism appointed to influential positions, Cameron was able to use their vagueness over means to cut the heart out of their social paternalism. This was evidenced most particularly in an interview given by Oliver Letwin to the *Daily Telegraph* on 23 December 2005. In this interview, which received much media attention, Letwin announced that the party would in future work to redistribute wealth. 'We do', he said, 'redistribute money and we should redistribute money.' It was clear, however, that this was a matter of 'empowerment' more than anything else. It was not that the gap between rich and poor would be addressed directly by a future Conservative government, but that general wealth creation was to be advocated above all else. This was a Soho wolf in Easterhouse clothing.

If Cameron was able to instigate a general campaign of attrition against the implications of Easterhouse principles, he was nevertheless still unwilling to begin a debate in the most controversial policy areas. While it was possible to undercut Willetts, Duncan Smith and Letwin on the NHS, for example, it was not so easy to challenge the still-powerful Easterhouse lobby on education. Given his pronouncements in the early stages of the leadership campaign, it would have been unsurprising for Cameron to have advanced the view that the best means of improving educational standards would be to introduce more 'choice' into the system. Through a voucher scheme or some similar means, parents would have greater scope to choose where their children would attend school, while schools would themselves have the capacity to select pupils according to predetermined criteria. The two forms of choice would have the effect of creating a primitive market environment within the educational system and thereby force up standards. To have advanced such a policy, however, would inevitably have brought Cameron into conflict with his shadow education secretary, Willetts, as well as with other Easterhouse modernisers. Although figures such as Willetts might have conceded that the institution of a market environment did indeed have the capacity to improve the quality of some schools, they would have also pointed out that it was impossible for all schools to improve as a result of this policy. Some schools would have to take the less able pupils rejected by other local establishments, thereby risking 'failure', jeopardising their future funding and hence being forced into a vicious spiral of decline. The weakest children would, in other words, effectively be denied even the standard of education they had previously received. For those attached to the cause of social justice, such a situation would be intolerable and no policy which would lead to such an educational environment could be accepted.

Had Cameron pursued the implications of his summer statements with respect to education, therefore, he would have led his party by a short path to civil war. At the same time, however, it was vitally important for the Conservative Party to take some stand on education. Polls had repeatedly demonstrated the significance of the issue to voters and if the party was to capitalise on the honeymoon period which followed Cameron's election, it had to distinguish itself tangibly from the Labour Party. The problem became particularly acute only days

after the leadership election was concluded, when the Labour government introduced an Education Bill which Tony Blair had identified as
being a crucial part of his political 'legacy'. Cameron had to act, but in
such a way that conflict was avoided.

The solution that was eventually hit upon was not novel, but it was
extremely effective. Wary of the difficulties of attempting to propose a
radically different set of policies in opposition to the Education Bill,
Cameron manoeuvred himself into a position in which he could expose
the divisions within the government while not actually making clear his
own party's stance. The Conservative Party, he said at Question Time,
would be delighted to support the government's Bill. He elaborated no
further. Although it appeared to be a rather bland and empty statement,
Cameron could not have delivered a more powerful blow.
Immediately, the Labour Party was thrown into disarray. Members of
Parliament who had already been sceptical of their party's proposals
were now moved to oppose the Bill openly. The horror of being on *the
same side as the Conservatives* shocked even John Prescott, the Deputy
Prime Minister, into declaring his rejection of the Bill in a much-
publicised interview in the *Sunday Telegraph*. The very real threat of
rebellion forced the government into a humiliating climbdown. A
critical piece of Blair's 'legacy' had been defeated and the Labour Party
revealed as disunited and rent by dissention. The Conservative Party, by
contrast, was left looking confident, assured and, above all else, united.

Cameron's approach to the Education Bill was based around nothing
other than triangulation. Afraid of dividing his own party, he had
assented to the proposals as a means of demonstrating the divisions of
the government. Knowing that the Bill was likely to be withdrawn, a
more detailed and potentially more damaging appraisal of its reforms
was not likely to be necessary. One of the most awkward and dangerous
policy debates had been avoided and a singular parliamentary success
had been delivered without substantial risk.

Although the Conservatives' approach to the Education Bill appears
impressive, it highlights the important point that Cameron's 'resolution'
was not a resolution at all. The rival interpretations of Conservatism
propounded by the Easterhouse and the Soho modernisers had not been
harmonised, nor had an agreement been reached. The contradictions

and tensions that had threatened to erupt into civil war in the late summer of 2005 remained. Indeed, given the extent to which each interpretation had been developed by the beginning of July 2005, it is questionable whether it would have been possible for the two to have been reconciled at all. Yet the strength of Cameron's leadership lay in the promise of resolution and the prospect of synthesis. His appointment of David Willetts, Oliver Letwin, Theresa May and Iain Duncan Smith to key posts and his use of Easterhouse language gave the impression of the formation of a new consensus. Easterhouse modernisers, seduced by the wiles of the cunning new leader, confidently expected that their commitment to social justice and their tolerance of higher public spending would be reflected in the party's programme for the future at the same time as Cameron was subtly neutralising the same principles. The substance of his extremely well-publicised announcements in December 2005 and January 2006 remained distinctly tied to the principles of Soho Conservatism, even though they were couched in quite different terms. The three-pronged strategy, comprising appeasement, attrition and triangulation, therefore allowed Cameron to reinvigorate the Conservatives as a party of opposition and to secure his own position without actually resolving any of the deep-rooted contradictions between the two interpretations of Conservatism. While it is fair to say that this made Cameron an effective opposition leader, it is, however, far from clear whether his strategy has either the capacity to work in the longer term or the potential to make the Conservative Party a viable party of government.

Prospects

Polls conducted in the aftermath of David Cameron's election as leader were unanimous in suggesting that his 'resolution' of Conservative tensions had increased the party's appeal amongst voters. In a survey conducted by ICM for the *Guardian* during the period 15–18 December 2005, 37 per cent of all those questioned said that they would support the Conservative Party if a general election was called the next day, compared to 36 per cent who would back Labour. When the same sample group were presented with a situation in which the three major parties were led by Cameron, Gordon Brown and Charles Kennedy, support for the Conservatives leapt to 41 per cent, while Labour remained static at 36 per cent and the Liberal Democrats dropped three points to 18 per cent. Even more impressively, not only did 56 per cent of people questioned say that Cameron was 'someone they could vote for' but 62 per cent indicated that he was the sort of person who could change the way they thought about the Conservative Party. Having only led Labour at the polls on one other occasion since 1997 (during the September 2000 petrol crisis), these figures certainly gave the impression both to senior party figures and to journalists that the Conservatives were experiencing something of a renaissance. In a leading article reacting to the ICM polling data, the *Guardian* stated on 20 December that 'New Labour's dominance is being threatened. . . . looking at all the recent polls as a whole, it seems clear that the Tories are back'. Scarcely able to contain his enthusiasm, Matthew Parris had echoed this view in the *Times* a few days before. Perhaps consciously evoking the Biblical language of prophecy, Parris emphatically declared that 'the Tories' hour has come'. Although rather more sceptical about the benefits of the realisation of such a prediction, Anatole Kaletsky grudgingly agreed that the Conservatives under Cameron did indeed appear set to return to government. Even amongst political activists in other parties, this interpretation was repeated. A YouGov poll published in the *Daily Telegraph* on 9 January 2006 showed that 68 per cent of Liberal Democrat members believed that Cameron's leadership of the Conservatives posed a 'very serious' threat to their party's prospects, clearly reflecting the widely held fear of substantial losses to the Conservatives at local elections held in May 2006 and the anticipated advent of a Conservative government in the appreciable future. The most surprising acknowledgement of the Conservative Party's apparent renaissance, however, came from the Prime Minister himself. In an interview in the *Observer* on 8 January 2006, Tony Blair unashamedly affirmed that Cameron's relocation of his party in the political 'centre ground' would give New Labour a 'real contest' at a future election and went on to expend great effort in refuting the claim that the Conservative Party was the 'natural party of government'.

Although the polling data is extremely striking, it must be treated with care. It is perhaps rather too easy to jump to conclusions on the basis of material which was, by its very nature, an anomaly in the period since 1997. Two facts are particularly important in dealing with the polling data from late 2005 and early 2006. First, the polls in question were conducted during a 'honeymoon' period following Cameron's election. The young, fresh-faced new leader had received an unprecedented level of favourable press attention both during the leadership election and after the result had been announced and it is perhaps no surprise that those questioned for polls during this time would have been influenced to some extent by this media image. Second, and possibly more important, the public were not particularly aware of the direction that the Conservative Party would pursue under Cameron's leadership, even by mid-January 2006. Specific policies were not announced, while the statements that were made gave few details and were couched in the broadest possible terms. In contrast to the precision that the Conservatives would be required to give during a general election campaign and the level of analysis and criticism that they would be likely to receive, the polls of the 'honeymoon' period were far more a reflection of the reception of a carefully presented image than of the party's long-term prospects.

While the Conservatives' image will be important in a future election, as Cameron suggested, it will only carry them so far. In order for the party to have a realistic chance of establishing itself as a potential government, it must develop a programme which is capable of winning support in those policy areas in which it was previously perceived as weak and which has the potential to take advantage of the collapse of Labour's social constituency. In assessing the extent to which Cameron's Conservative Party would be able to achieve this, it is necessary to examine the relationship between the party's policies at the 2005 general election and the electorate's reaction to them, before going on to consider how feasible it would be for the areas of weakness to be transformed into sources of strength.

In the leadup to the 2005 general election, MORI conducted a series of polls which tested the importance of certain issues in determining the way in which people would vote. The ten issues which were revealed as the most significant were, in declining order: health; immigration; education; law and order; defence; pensions; economic management; housing; poverty and unemployment; and taxation. When people were asked which party they believed had the best policy on each of these issues, the Conservatives were considered superior to both Labour and the Liberal Democrats with respect to immigration, law and order, defence and taxation. With regard to policy on pensions, they were held to be slightly less preferable to Labour by those who regarded the issue as important, but were perceived as marginally more preferable overall. On the management of the economy, health, education, housing and poverty and unemployment, Labour commanded a clear lead over each of the other parties.

It is always difficult to interpret such polls, particularly given that there is no means of telling exactly what is actually the primary determinant of voting behaviour and the impossibility of establishing whether the truth is being told, but nevertheless some implications can be drawn from the data that MORI collected.

First, those policy areas for which the Conservatives were perceived as having the best approach were those which have been viewed as its 'strong' areas for many years. Low tolerance of crime, a commitment to maintaining the power of Britain's armed forces and a sceptical view of the value of a receptive attitude towards immigration have been policies which have remained relatively unchanged through the course of every election since the 1970s. Similarly, the party has long been viewed as the party of low taxation, particularly since the premiership of Margaret Thatcher. These are areas which touch closely on those most fundamental of Conservative beliefs and they are policies which have not seriously been challenged by either the Soho or the Easterhouse modernisers, despite their differences of emphasis.

Second, Labour's success in achieving greater approval than the Conservatives for its policies on health, education, housing and poverty and unemployment have coincided with a marked difference in the presentation of their manifesto pledges. Health and education are two areas which are worth looking at in some detail, not least because they were the first and third most important factors determining the way in which people would vote.

In detailing their approach to the NHS in their 2005 manifesto, the Conservatives began from the premise that it was 'too impersonal, too inflexible, too centralised and too bureaucratic to respond to the needs of patients'. Although it made a specific promise to match Labour's spending on the NHS, the manifesto emphasised the role of choice in 'driving up standards'. The Labour manifesto contained nothing which was opposed to 'choice'; indeed, it specifically promised to give 'more power to patients over their own treatment and over their own health'. It did, however, begin its policies on health from the premise that the centralised provision of care should be maintained. As the manifesto put it, 'this means defeating those who would dismantle the NHS'. Increases in hospital capacity, improvements in the quality of treatment and the potential for more specialised care centres were stressed greatly. The point is that while Labour's policy actually differed very little from the Conservatives', it was presented as committing the party to the preservation of a centralised NHS that could be improved by state means more than by any other method.

In education, the substantive policies were the same. Each party promised higher funding, more teachers, smaller class sizes and some involvement from private companies. Yet the two manifestos differed greatly in the emphasis they put on their policy. Again, the Conservatives stressed the importance of choice for parents, but complemented this by giving tremendous weight to the maintenance of discipline in schools. The Labour Party, however, made a great virtue of its communitarian approach. The potential for all to benefit, the promise to parents that 'where there is no improvement there will be intervention' and the pledge to support and reward teachers were aspects which were highlighted particularly forcefully. Indeed, Labour's lengthy chapter on education began and ended with the statement that 'our country has been held back by an education system that excelled for the privileged few but let down the majority'. It was not that Labour actually opposed anything that the Conservatives were suggesting, least of all with respect to funding and the involvement of the private sector, but that the crucial differences lie in the presentation. While the Conservatives chose to present themselves as tough on discipline but liberal on choice, the Labour Party chose to project an image of itself as a party with a social conscience determined to eradicate inequality in the provision of education.

Labour's great success at the 2005 general election in these policy areas was presentational. Although the substance of their manifesto differed very little from that of the Conservatives, they effectively created the impression that there was a great gulf dividing them. Labour's strategy was double-pronged. On the one hand, they presented their motivation as being communitarian. On the other hand, they presented the Conservatives as being unreconstructed Thatcherites whose attachment to decentralisation and privatisation threatened the quality of care that could be offered by key public services. Implicitly reminding voters of the perceived failure of privatisation, Labour suggested that to trust health and education to the Conservatives was to invite a more damaging repeat of the fate of British Rail.

These implications are of great importance to the effect of David Cameron's 'resolution' of the tension between the Soho and Easterhouse modernisers. The 'wolf in sheep's clothing' approach – by which the liberal economics of Soho Conservatism are introduced under the guise of the social paternalism of the Easterhouse faction – may be an effective means of conducting opposition during the 'honeymoon' months, but it is far from clear that the distinctively liberal policies which it engenders will be able to deliver tangible electoral benefits on their own. A repeated commitment to low taxation, for example, would almost certainly not win much in the way of meaningful support at a future general election. This issue was only important to 6 per cent of voters in the spring of 2005 and the Conservatives' dominance in this area seems almost unassailable in any case. Increasing the profile of low taxation would therefore only consolidate their position with a relatively small number of people. By the same token, it is unlikely that stressing their commitment to reducing government involvement in public services and giving an even freer rein to the effect of the market would do them any good either. Such an approach has little chance – barring the advent of a new recession – of denting the government's considerable lead in economic management. What is more, this liberal-economic stance seems likely to increase the inhibitions of voters and to give credence to Labour's caricature of the

Conservatives as being an even more dangerous threat to public services than Thatcher, a point that Cameron himself acknowledged in his repeated but unconvincing disavowal of his party's earlier policies on healthcare.

MORI's polls indicate that if the Conservative Party is to become a viable government of the future in the eyes of the electorate, then it should not emphasise its attachment to low taxation and private involvement in public services but concentrate more effectively on propounding a more centrist and paternalistic series of social policies. The findings of surveys conducted in the leadup to the 2005 general election demonstrate clearly that the British public are more inclined towards the assurance that is provided by a communitarian approach than the perceived risks of free-market economics. The reassurance of social concern is capable of convincing many former Labour voters of the value of Conservatism as a real political alternative, all the more so when the collapse of Labour's social constituency is considered. Those who have turned away from the Labour Party, particularly in its heartlands, appear to have repudiated their earlier voting patterns not because they have ceased to believe in 'Labour' values, but because they have become disenchanted with the party itself. What has kept them from voting Conservative and has persuaded them to vote for the Liberal Democrats or other parties in the past is the belief that Conservatism, particularly with a liberal-economic focus, is deeply opposed to those communitarian values that they continue to hold dear.

It is true that Cameron's use of Easterhouse language in the early months of his leadership will certainly help in this respect and if this could be used across all areas of social policy in the same manner, then it would be possible to make a reasonable case for the Conservatives' ability to reclaim a sizeable number of votes from both Labour and the Liberal Democrats at a future general election. Yet, as Cameron's own strategy demonstrates, it is manifestly not possible for him to sustain the pretence indefinitely. If gains are going to be made from Labour and the Liberal Democrats, it is necessary to give greater substance to claims of social concern and to adopt a larger portion of Easterhouse communitarianism into the party's social policies, particularly with respect to education, pensions, deprivation and unemployment. The security of the Conservatives' future, in other words, depends on the reality of social justice as a guiding principle in policy formation. It is precisely this, however, that is in question when Cameron's leadership is examined.

In opposition, with an election some years away, it is possible for the Conservative Party to operate in 'neutral' with regard to the most electorally significant issues in social policy. Internally, the Easterhouse modernisers may be controlled effectively through the continued deployment of appeasement, attrition and triangulation, while the language of social concern may be used to give weight to the announcement of various policy revisions. This approach has been shown to be effective but, as has previously been stated, its strength rests on the promise of resolution that it offers and this promise can only be sustained unfulfilled so long as an election is not imminent. As a general election nears, the party will be put under pressure to deliver a complete package of social policies. This will inexorably bring Cameron to a fork in the road. Such a package must necessarily have public appeal and take account of the fundamental weaknesses of the 2005 manifesto. In order to produce this, however, Cameron may choose to do one of two things. On the one hand, social policy could be based around the liberal economics of Soho Conservatism, but expressed as the best means of delivering social justice. Thus, in the same manner as Labour did at the 2005 general election, the Conservative Party could propose the introduction of an internal market to the NHS, for example, while stating their determination to 'leave no one behind' in the provision of high-quality healthcare. If well presented, such an approach to policy is likely to deliver the desired effect and could, indeed, result in an increased support for the party from the fragmented remains of Labour's traditional social constituency. The problem with such a 'resolution' is not electoral, however, but party political. In pursuing this course of action, Cameron would at once alienate the Easterhouse modernisers and remove his best means of gaining their loyalty. Even if the party were to be returned to government with this attitude towards social policy, it is likely that Cameron would be faced with the prospect of having to contain a groundswell of dissatisfaction that could prove to be a weakness comparable to that experienced by Tony Blair during the debates on the Terror Bill and the Education Bill in late 2005. This should not be underestimated. Conservative MPs have never been afraid of rebelling against the party whip and under Michael Howard's leadership this tendency was as visible as ever. As a result of studies conducted by Philip Cowley and Mark Stuart, it has become clear that during the period 2003–2005 Conservative MPs were most willing to defy the whip over social issues; in a number of cases the party had to allow a free vote to avoid the appearance of a rebellion. Although the subjects over which the splits were most evident have little direct relationship to the tension between liberal economics and social paternalism, an analysis of the manner in which specific MPs voted reveals a striking division of personalities which reflects closely the composition of the Soho and Easterhouse factions.

However, it would be perfectly plausible for Cameron genuinely to base his party's social policy on the principles of Easterhouse Conservatism. The NHS could, for example, be maintained as a wholly public service with better funding and the state could initiate a series of direct-action schemes to combat inner-city deprivation. Such an approach would not only deliver *the same* electoral benefits as a more superficial attitude, but would also have the additional advantage of fully and effectively integrating Easterhouse modernisers into a party led by a Soho Conservative. The disadvantage of this approach, however, is that it would force the party to abandon its commitment to lowering taxation and controlling public spending. This is no small point. Not only would it compromise the most distinctive feature of Cameron's Soho Conservatism – the Conservatism which formed the basis of his platform during the leadership election – but it would also erode the party's capacity to present itself as economically sensible. Although it is questionable whether the Conservatives would necessarily lose all of their substantial advantage in polls with respect to taxation even if they abandoned their pledge to lower taxes, this would prove to be a major weakness in an election which is likely to be fought against a Labour Party led by Gordon Brown, who has successfully given himself an air of economic prudence.

Although it is impossible to determine accurately which of these two eventualities will come to pass, one cannot avoid the conclusion that in either case the Conservative Party is in a poor position to overcome the weaknesses of the 2005 manifesto and to inspire greater confidence with respect to social policy. Cameron's capacity to deliver a programme which will compensate for his party's previous electoral inadequacies is limited by the extent of the divisions within his party and by his own reluctance to attempt a compelling resolution to an ongoing problem. Inevitably this casts a shadow over an assessment of the party's prospects at a future general election. The weakness of the party's social policy must necessarily compromise its electoral prospects. While many polls suggest that there is a better chance of the next government being Conservative than at any point since 1997, the party's ability to achieve that end is not as great as it might be, and its capacity to retain what unity it possesses is in question.

The weakness of social policy – what might reasonably be termed the Achilles heel of the Conservative Party – has arisen as a direct result of recent political history. More specifically, it is the necessary consequence of Labour's mastery of triangulation. Although by 2005 the Labour Party was no longer displaying its earlier skill in out-manoeuvring its opponents, the dilemma with which the Conservative Party was faced had arisen many years previously, out of the wreckage of the 1997 general election. Indeed, in many senses, it could compellingly be argued that although the Achilles heel of Cameron's Conservative Party was most clearly revealed in the months following the 2005 general election, it had first been exposed during the leadership of William Hague. It was in this period of shock following Blair's first landslide victory that the conditions were created for the emergence of two radically different and virtually irreconcilable conceptions of the same political creed. The failure of subsequent leaders to challenge the New Politics effectively and to take advantage of Labour's already crumbling social constituency merely compounded the problem. If, therefore, Cameron is to be held to account for failing to resolve the tensions which exist within the Conservative Party, then it must simultaneously be admitted that he is simply atoning for the sins of his political forebears who suffered so grievously at the hands of the New Politics. This is essentially an historical point, but its implications are far reaching. In failing to transcend the weaknesses engendered by its history since 1997, the Conservative Party is in serious danger not only of jeopardising its long-term integrity but also of failing to capitalise on the collapse of Labour's social constituency. As a prisoner of its own past, the Conservative Party may miss the opportunity with which it has been provided by electoral developments and, as will be shown in later chapters, at the same time risk leaving unaddressed the most pressing issues of recent British history.

4

The Liberal Democrats and the New Politics

If triangulation has undermined the values and ideology of the two main parties, loosening their appeal to the British electorate, then it is appropriate to ask whether it has damaged the two-party system altogether. If the Labour and Conservative parties have emerged from triangulation scarred and thus deeply unattractive, then it would be reasonable to assume that Britain's third party has profited in the process. This chapter studies the capacity of the Liberal Democrats to emerge as a new force in politics and to create a whole new discourse involving three or more parties.

This is precisely what they appeared to do in the 2005 election. Long after his sudden and brutal removal from office, Charles Kennedy still remained credited with much of their success. Even those who later benefited from his resignation were careful to appear respectful. Sir Menzies Campbell, speaking on the BBC's *Question Time* on 9 April 2006, though insisting flatly that 'a point had come that, for his own interests and those of his party, that he should step aside', stated that 'Charles Kennedy enjoys great affection . . . because he delivered the best result for over 80 years.' Simon Hughes similarly praised his 'leadership' in his commencement address.

On 18 July 2005, shortly after the general election, Kennedy gave a speech at Westminster in which he reflected upon his party's rationale and the strategy that would still earn him praise six months later from the very people that would eventually conspire to remove him. Many of its phrases touched upon the key themes developed in the first few chapters of this book: the death of ideology at the hands of triangulation and the rise of a 'New Politics' based upon competition for title of 'best manager' of society and the economy.

Kennedy spoke to a group emboldened by a rising percentage within the polls. It was a Liberal Democratic movement stripped of beards and sandals, a movement that was the apparent master of the New Politics. He told his audience:

> We are at our best and we do our best when we are positive and united. People respond well to that, not least because these days politics has become less intensely ideological and needs to be more solution based. As we Liberal Democrats advance solutions they need, of course, to be based on sound principles and a considered philosophy. That's why opinion polls, in 2001 and 2005 alike, confirm the public as scoring ours to be the best campaign.

This vision of triangulation, the denial of the 'ideological' and the embrace of the 'practical', was not Kennedy's alone. In a speech full of bold contradiction declaring his candidacy, Mark Oaten echoed those sentiments, but argued that the Liberal Democrats had hampered themselves by not moving quickly enough to eschew associations with ideology:

> We need to move forward to create a truly modern, 21st-century liberal party which people out there in the country can identify with and with popular policies that they want to vote for . . . This contest is not just about modernising the party, but it's about the issue of whether it is left or right . . . and I believe that in fact those are the wrong phrases. We need now to merge those ideas together.

His rival Campbell advertised himself as having 'no time for the media-driven view that we must either lurch to the left or lunge to the right. Given the progressive liberal agenda that Liberal Democrats represent . . . [I view] these terms as meaningless.'

But within the leadership campaign there remained a tension that made a mockery of Oaten's and Campbell's appeal to the new centre ground. It was partly fostered by Hughes's campaign, rudely and proudly egalitarian, populist and unashamedly left wing. His speech to the Meeting the Challenge conference in London in January 2006 identified economic and democratic inequality as his primary issue:

> Over two and a half decades of Thatcherite and New Labour governments, Britain has steadily become a less equal and less fair society. Inequality in wealth is still increasing, as are inequalities in standards of health. Under New Labour, rates of social mobility have actually fallen . . . unfettered free economics brings social division, gross income and opportunity inequality, and political chasm.

It was a speech that demands comparison with anti-Blairite critiques of the hard left and even of the Respect Coalition.

There was also tension in the rhetoric of those candidacies that did strive for the centre ground. They were accused of denying the obvious. Even if the leadership contenders regarded terms of 'left' and 'right' as 'meaningless', the national media apparently regarded them as at least convenient. The *Guardian* ran a headline on Friday 13 January 2006 that quoted, or paraphrased, Campbell as declaring that he would take the Liberal Democrats to 'the left of Labour'. Confronted in a BBC interview about the article on the 14th, Campbell tetchily retorted that he didn't 'think it is left wing to want to lift people out of poverty'. That same day, the *Telegraph* dubbed Oaten as 'right wing' and about Hughes declined to mince its words altogether. It opened an unflattering interview with a frank description of him as a 'sandal-wearing leftie'.

This tension did not just begin with the leadership contest. It was present in Kennedy's speech in Westminster. It was a speech that was perhaps indicative of the Liberal Democrats' shortcomings, unconsciously predicting that they might not yet be as ready to reap the benefits of triangulation as the polls indicated. The problem for Kennedy was one of pitching his party to the correct audience. That day in Westminster he stepped closer to claiming the title of Britain's dominant left-of-centre party as he tried to steal many of Labour's clothes:

> Nearly a century ago, the greatest reforming government that this country had ever experienced set out to change the face of Britain. That Liberal government of 1906 took head on the issues of poverty and welfare provision . . . Asquith and Lloyd George established the principles and began the construction of the British welfare state that emerged fully after the Second World War. The National Health Service, with its doctrine of universal service, was largely the result of the work of the great Liberal Lord Beveridge.

Kennedy, however, reiterated that consistent theme: that his party was above ideology, 'neither left nor right'. Simply sensible. Nevertheless the argument that the origins of twentieth-century social reform lay not with Labour but with the 1906 Liberal governments would prove to be a centrepiece of Hughes's candidacy. At the Meeting the Challenge conference on 14 January 2006, the first party forum the leadership hopefuls attended, he reminded his audience: 'Asquith, Lloyd George and Churchill laid the foundations of the modern welfare state, bringing in old-age pensions, national insurance, labour exchanges and redistributive taxation. They had the courage to build a more equal and fairer society.' Kennedy was attempting to balance an appeal to a centre ground free of ideology while addressing a heritage apparently steeped in egalitarian populism that appealed to the left of his party. The tensions within his leadership were not merely personal but indicative of some greater paradox or conflict in the ranks.

A centre without an ideology and the New Politics

But to return to Kennedy's hypothesis of the roots of his victory, it is tempting to agree with his verdict. Indeed, the speech was highly significant for analysing the potential of a third party to emerge in the wake of triangulation. Declining loyalty, based in the past upon identification with either Labour or Conservative 'values', has created a sea of floating voters. Arguably with the death of ideology that Kennedy identified in his speech, politics is now being fought on the Liberal Democrats' home territory. In the fight for victory in the overcrowded centre, the Liberal Democrats have an apparent advantage. For generations they have claimed to carry the banner for those that disagree that government should be put to an ideological purpose: Conservatives disquieted by aggressive aspects of its economic and social policy and natural Labour supporters unenamoured of class war. Lacking a clear ideological identity has apparently permitted them to fight a war on two fronts, and with some success. They maintain domination of the South-West on a Eurosceptic, soft conservative ticket and won a by-election in Brent East in 2004 with an aggressively anti-war stance. They have a remarkable ability to remain both apparently moderate and centrist and to outflank their opponents, moving to the left in London and the north and to the right in the south.

Moreover, the Liberal Democrats are well placed to benefit from the shift in politics from national to local emphasis. They are notoriously good local campaigners, focusing upon regional issues and establishing themselves as the party most concerned with local politics. An example of this was shown in the Cheadle by-election of 2005. Patsy Calton, the Liberal Democrat MP who had held the seat since 2001, increased her majority from 33 to over 4,000 by establishing a reputation as a hard-working constituency MP. After her sudden death days after the 2005 general election, the Liberal Democrats once again ran a campaign based on local rather than national issues, picking up on themes such as the state of the roads, hanging baskets and crime. But the Tories showed a notable awareness of the significance of local issues, Michael Howard commenting, 'We have been doing a lot more of that. Elections have become much more local in their content. People [increasingly] want a local champion.' After a rape took place that shocked the town, the Conservatives distributed a leaflet that attacked the crime-fighting record of Mark Hunter, the Liberal Democrat candidate, above a headline describing the incident. Nonetheless Hunter, chair of the local council, held the seat.

What has made the Liberal Democrats remarkable, however, has been their ability to attract support both from those who favour the policies that result from triangulation and from the voters who feel alienated from the process of their creation. In short they have fashioned an electorate out of centrists and the disaffected left. As economic debate has subsided and social issues have gained in significance, so many groups have left the Labour Party over issues of conscience and have found themselves drawn to the third party. Indeed, it is wrong to analyse the success of the Liberal Democrats in isolation, for it is in fact symptomatic of the triumph of triangulation. With the death of ideology the public has began to afford the party greater attention. Their historic ability to outflank their opponents has been given ample opportunity to flourish. It could even be argued that the Liberal Democrats have not simply stood still in the last eight years and allowed floating voters to come to them. Instead they too have triangulated, offering policies on single issues designed to appeal to those affected by the most traumatic political shift in the last decade, the loss of Labour's materialist discourse and its perceived commitment to social progress and reform.

The party has shifted in some areas in order to benefit from the rupture within the Labour coalition. Currently, the Liberal Democrats are credited as Britain's main anti-Iraq war party. This is in fact evidence of the very 'spinning' which the public regularly credit the party for eschewing, as the front bench's policy was in fact opposition only if the coalition forces failed to win the United Nations' backing. Moreover the public has, in several constituencies, punished sitting or prospective Labour MPs despite their complete agreement with Liberal Democrat policy. In Cambridge Ann Campbell lost her seat despite resigning from the government over the war and in the 2004 Brent East by-election Labour candidate Robert Evans lost despite his public opposition to it. Liberal Democrat populism has secured them members of the old Labour coalition potentially for elections to come, notably students and young Asians. But this support was not a reflection of attraction to a tradition of Liberal Democrat pacifism. On the contrary, when Paddy Ashdown (a keen supporter of the second Gulf War) was leader the party readily endorsed the bombing of Serbia and military engagement in Sierra Leone. The Liberal Democrats themselves have moved in response to triangulation, creating a double-pronged strategy of selling themselves both as the natural party of centrist 'solutions-based' government and as a soft-left alternative to Labour. The degree to which this contradictory strategy is a reflection of divisions within the party and the extent to which it may eventually hamper a Liberal Democrat electoral breakthrough are at the heart of this chapter.

Again, it is important to stress that this is a result of the Labour Party's triangulation. This phenomenon has been mirrored in the growing success of the third parties in US presidential elections in the last thirty years, demonstrating once more on an international scale the death of materialist ideology within capitalist democracies. Third parties have always been most successful in American presidential elections when the Democrats have gone through a process of triangulation. Indeed third-

party politics has escaped authoritative analysis both sides of the
Atlantic, despite its quiet but steady rise in the past few decades,
consistently at the expense of the Democrats. In Minnesota, a state that
has been alone in voting Democrat in every presidential election since
1976, the party of the toiling masses was deemed so unvoteworthy that
in 1998 it lost the gubernatorial race to an ex-pro wrestling star, Jesse
Ventura, running on a 'Reform' ticket. Nationally, the most obvious
and recent examples of third-party presidential election insurgency
were Ross Perot (who took 19 per cent in 1992 and 8.4 per cent in
1996) and Ralph Nader (the share was small – only 3 per cent in 2000
– but enough to lose the Democrats Florida).

But the Democrats first experimented with a variety of triangulation
in 1976. Jimmy Carter's administration was ill defined of purpose,
desperately unsuited to the moment and unable to exploit triangulation
effectively or even consciously, but he was the political model for Bill
Clinton and the 'New' Democrats. He campaigned for President as a
centrist, with strong religious values and a distrust of big government.
He even won plaudits in England, where Labour modernisers such as
Peter Jay fêted him for his attempt to move his party to the centre. His
strategy had some success in the election of 1976, although Eugene
McCarthy, standing as an independent Liberal Democrat, came close to
losing him the vital state of New York with his 15 per cent of the vote,
until he was removed from the ballot paper. But Carter's fiscal
conservatism proved disastrous in 1980. His insistence upon eschewing
government intervention in the economy and his lukewarm social
liberalism had alienated the Democratic base of voters. It was a warning
to left-wing parties that reject their own history and values. Activism fell
sharply, many liberal groups refused to endorse him and turnout was
low. In the 1980 election the shift from the Democrats to the
Republicans was titanic and largest among groups traditionally
associated with the liberal coalition. In particular, a significant 15 per
cent of Hispanics switched to voting Republican. History has often
blamed the 1980 Republican landslide on the popularity of opponent
Ronald Reagan and a rising conservatism within the American public.
But the Republican candidate was not much more popular at all.
Reagan had not yet presided over a boom, was associated with what his

own running mate, George Bush Sr, described as 'voodoo economics' and had a very public love affair with intercontinental ballistic missiles. Carter was beaten by himself and the margin of Republican victory in many states was measured in defecting Hispanics, Jews, women, young people, union members and the white poor.

The result of a triangulating left-wing party fighting it out with an unpopular opposition was the third-party candidacy of John B. Anderson. History has not been kind to Anderson, because his final tally of 6.6 per cent of the national vote was later overshadowed by Perot's candidacies. But before Perot, Anderson's was the second most successful third-party run in American post-war history. Until the last few weeks of the campaign he was registering between 20 and 30 per cent in the polls and on election day won millions of votes across the northeast. Anderson was a liberal Republican who had entered the primaries and been soundly beaten. But commentators recognised that the primary electorate were far to the right of the country and Anderson had scored well enough in national polls to justify a third-party run. What was fascinating about the Anderson campaign was that it bore close comparison with that of the modern Liberal Democrats. In most regards Anderson was stubbornly centrist. He supported a balanced budget, low taxes and fiscal discipline. But he became known for his more liberal pronouncements, opposing military activity in Iran, taking a pro-choice stance on abortion and endorsing environmentalism and conservation. Ultimately, he attracted support from a mixture of moderate Republicans and liberal Democrats. He scored best among liberal supporters of the old Democratic coalition, particularly amongst students and Jewish communities.

A comparison with Anderson is valuable not just because he too mixed a centrist image with an appeal to left-wing groups but because his campaign was a product of triangulation. He gained support because traditional Democratic groups did not like the abjuration of ideology that Carter espoused and because moderate Republicans were unenthused by an apparently incompetent opposition nominee. Traditional voting patterns broke down, in some regards dramatically, and Anderson, regarded in polling as 'new', 'positive' and 'moderate', benefited enormously. But equally importantly, when ideology reasserted itself four years later Anderson declined to enter the presidential race. In 1984 the Republicans had a popular candidate and the Democrats returned to the traditional liberal fold, along with most of its regular ethnic and interest group support. Anderson was a victim of circumstance; as the candidates returned to the politics of ideology and the electoral bases to their respective parties, his campaign was halted.

The Liberal Democrats are now at a turning point in their history. This has in part been forced by scandal, evidence of the new attention that success in the polls attracts from the media. It is also a dynamic to which the British third party has always been intensely sensitive. In the elections of 1974 the Liberal Party appeared to be groping towards electoral significance and even coalition government, but after Jeremy Thorpe appeared in court in 1978, charged with conspiracy to murder, the following year's general election vote declined dramatically. In 1992 Paddy Ashdown's affair with his secretary was at least partly responsible for the recently formed Liberal Democratic Party's poor performance at the polls. A third party is sensitive to scandal because its leader is usually the sole media attention that the movement receives and because moral outrage strips away its claim to offer an alternative to corrupt main-stream politics. But the nature of Charles Kennedy's fall from grace and of the subsequent leadership election revealed that the real problem facing the Liberal Democrats is the extent to which they are ideologically divided. The ill-fated candidacy of Mark Oaten was telling in this regard. He was encouraged to enter the contest by MPs purely because they wanted to present a challenge to Menzies Campbell, to open a debate within the party and to offer an ideological alternative. However, his support did not last and those that urged him to run failed to campaign openly for him. They felt a debate was necessary, but did not yet know exactly what to say and did not actually favour the chosen messenger. His candidacy lasted just nine days.

It is broadly accepted that Kennedy's fall was not dictated simply by health problems, but by frustration with his message, leadership and attempts to pitch the party in a leftward direction. It made clear that the Liberal Democrats are reliant, as was John Anderson in 1980, upon certain political circumstances to attract a diversity of supporters. They are the creatures of triangulation in that they attract voters that are disenchanted with its effect upon the government and opposition. The purpose of this chapter is to evaluate the long-term potential of the Liberal Democrats to become a powerful force in the post-Cold War era. An understanding of their potential rests on an understanding of what their structure as a party leaves them capable of doing politically. Kennedy spoke at Westminster of the death of ideology and the necessity for politics to become 'solutions based'. At face value the Liberal Democrats are poised to benefit from this sea change and it would appear that they already have. However, it is our contention that the Liberal Democrats are not as well suited to the New Politics as their opinion poll ratings suggest. To understand why not, it is appropriate first to evaluate the gulf between what the public regards the Liberal Democrats as being, their responses to their actual policies and the true nature of the liberal/social-democratic coalition that makes up the party. Let us return to the point before the party divided to understand its initial success, to the 2005 general election and its moment of relative glory.

Perception and reality

The public knew surprisingly little about the fashionable party of 2005. An analysis of British response to the Liberal Democrat platform goes some way to illuminating the darkness. Tiredness with the other two parties had produced, on general issues of party credibility, something approaching infatuation. The Liberal Democrats were voted in MORI opinion polls as the party most likely to keep its promises. It was the most compassionate party, beating Labour in 'care for the people in real need in Britain' by 30 per cent to 20 per cent. The public felt that both the Labour and Conservative parties were prepared to 'offer anything to win votes' by overwhelming pluralities of 40 per cent and 45 per cent respectively. Only 19 per cent felt the same about the Liberal Democrats. It was the party least out of touch with ordinary people's thinking (by just 8 per cent to the Tories' 32 per cent) and the least dominated by personality (by 6 per cent to Labour's 37 per cent), a quality frowned upon by the British people in 2005.

This reaction, so significantly more positive than that shown towards the government and opposition, was based on a profound ignorance of Liberal Democrat policy. The party received by far the largest number of 'Don't know' or 'No opinion' responses in MORI polls throughout the election. In one sample, 9 per cent said they had no knowledge of Labour Party policy, contrasted with 23 per cent for the Liberal Democrats. Many were contradictory in their responses. They liked the party a great deal, but did not feel passionately about it. By only 6 per cent to the Tories' 17 per cent did the public feel 'so strongly opposed to the Party that I discourage others from voting for it without being asked'. But a striking 56 per cent said that 'if someone asked my opinion I would be neutral about voting for the [Liberal Democrat] Party'.

Moreover, what people did actually know of its policies they didn't like. With the very notable exceptions of Iraq and the environment, the public voted that the Liberal Democrats had the worst stance of all three parties on every single issue. One opinion poll carried out for the *Evening Standard* in April 2005 did not bode well for election day. For instance, on 'managing the economy' 53 per cent felt Labour was best and 23 per cent the Conservatives, but a desultory 4 per cent preferred the Liberal Democrats. On the key social issues, which thanks to triangulation quietly dominated the campaign, the Liberal Democrats performed appallingly. On law and order 38 per cent felt the Tories were most capable, Labour 26 per cent and the Liberal Democrats just 5 per cent. Interestingly, on asylum Labour and the Liberal Democrats almost equally divided a core liberal vote. Of the 19 per cent of the voters that did not approve of Tory policy, 11 per cent preferred Labour and 8 per cent the Liberal Democrats. Finally, the Liberal Democrats did badly even on the flagship areas of their campaign. They campaigned assiduously for a 'citizen's pension' but were favoured on pension issues by only 12 per cent of the public. They also ran a crusade to abolish council tax, but received only 10 per cent of support on tax issues to Labour's 30 per cent.

The most immediate experience people have of a party is of its leader and again the public was not impressed at all. Tony Blair was felt to be a capable leader by 34 per cent, Kennedy by just 18 per cent. Blair was thought to be capable in a crisis by 19 per cent, Kennedy by a shocking 2 per cent. Oddly, Blair bucked his party's trends by being voted the leader who most understood Britain's problems, with Kennedy trailing five points behind him, and he was also felt to have the most charisma. Most damning, Kennedy was felt by just 11 per cent to understand world problems and by a plurality of 35 per cent to be too inexperienced for the job. More positively, Kennedy mirrored his party in two respects. He was liked enormously, being voted considerably more honest than his competitors, far more in touch with ordinary voters and far less likely to talk down to people. But the second respect was a striking degree of ignorance of who he was and what he stood for. Some 23 percent felt that they did not know enough about Kennedy to pass comment on him.

What was attracting people to the Liberal Democrats? Remarkably, the party seemed to have achieved something Labour never did during the 1980s: an ability to appear both compassionate and competent. The British people felt that Kennedy's party cared deeply about them and their problems, but was not socially divisive or even socialist. The Liberal Democrats were felt to represent all classes better than Labour or the Tories. It was the party least likely to be voted too extreme for government (2 per cent to the Conservative's 14 per cent) and the party most voted moderate, by 31 per cent. Its nearest rival, the Labour Party, had just 16 per cent. It was also felt to have 'the most sensible policies' by 27 per cent to just 18 per cent for Labour and 17 per cent for the Conservatives. A remarkable victory, considering how much the public registered disapproval of their policies when they were discussed individually. What was striking about MORI's research was the similarity between responses to the Labour Party and the Conservatives and the very different response to the Liberal Democrats. Labour and the Tories were felt to be too fractious by 22 per cent and 23 per cent of respondents respectively. The Liberal Democrats were voted so by only 5 per cent.

But what was even more remarkable was once more the disparity between public perception and reality. The British people perceived the Liberal Democrats as being moderate in policy and united in activism. Although it is difficult to precisely define 'moderate', it is possible to detect elements of radicalism within the Liberal Democrats at least to an extent that rivals Labour and the Conservatives. Its conferences still decide policy based upon debate on the conference floor and the thrashing out of a consensus. In 2000, for instance, this process edged the party towards embracing overt republicanism, a constitutional radicalism never once adopted by the Labour Party and which only ever bordered on being fashionable among Bennite activists in the early 1980s. The party unanimously voted to remove the Queen as head of the Church of England and defender of the faith, although further steps to limit her powers were narrowly voted down. But republicanism is just the tip of the iceberg. The party has also voted to scrap mandatory life sentences for murder and for a second serious sexual or violent crime; to abolish faith, grammar and specialist schools; to provide compulsory sex education for seven-year-olds; and, perhaps most significantly, to remove the right-to-buy policy on council homes.

The last policy is most interesting as it goes to the heart of the second misperception that the public held of the Liberal Democrats in 2005: that they are united. While disunity was most apparent in the 2006 leadership contest, it must be stressed that it was not merely manufactured for the sake of defining candidates and creating oppositional discourses. It has been present throughout the party's brief history. In 2004 two events caused a minor media storm and highlighted the split within the Liberal Democrat ranks. The first was the competition between Simon Hughes and Lembit Öpik for the party's presidency, a battle that quickly became symbolic of the struggle between the left and the right to frame party ideology. The second was the row that erupted over the publishing of the *Orange Book*, a series of essays that detailed policy alternatives – alternatives, that is, to the centre-left thinking prevalent among activists. Much attention focused on an essay by Treasury spokesman David Laws on the future of the NHS, but its tone was consistent with all the others. Nick Clegg wrote an essay that bordered on Euroscepticism, Edward Davey questioned the benefits of ballooning state bureaucracy and Vince Cable wrote of the potentially damaging effects of 'politicising' the economy. The arguments over the spirit of the *Orange Book* spilled out on to the conference floor. A heated debate erupted over the party's commitment to maintaining a health service free at the point of delivery. Laws urged the party to consider a private health insurance scheme to replace some NHS support and was angrily shouted down. One speaker warned him, 'We don't need three right-wing parties in Britain . . . We don't need to follow New Labour to the right . . . We remain at the progressive centre-left.' Interestingly, the split over public health funding delineated along geographic lines: Laws represented Yeovil, in the West Country, and the speaker was a delegate from the Camberwell & Peckham constituency, in London.

The left demonstrated an equal ability to cause controversy when in 2000 they put a motion to conference to restore the link between earnings and pensions. Had it passed it would have left a multi-million-pound hole in the party's election sums. Once more the split was along geographic as well as ideological lines. Archy Kirkwood, the MP for Roxburgh & Berwickshire, spoke for the restoration of the link. He was opposed by the full weight of the leadership, including Laws, Paddy Ashdown and the spokesman on social security in the upper house, Lord Russell. The first two represented South West areas and with the exception of Laws all had clear links to the Liberal Party of twenty years previously.

The cause of the 2006 leadership contest lay in the history of the Liberal Democrats: a history of two distinct halves. In the early 1980s a group of four Labour ex-Cabinet members, Shirley Williams, Bill Rodgers, David Owen and Roy Jenkins, formed the Social Democratic Party, a soft-left alternative to their old party. They negotiated an alliance for the sake of electoral convenience with the Liberal Party, then under the leadership of David Steel. At the end of the 1980s the parties finally merged, having failed to break the two-party system while they maintained separate identities. This has created an artificial partnership, defined in part by the acrimony within which it was formed. The refusal of Owen, by then the titular head of the SDP, to accept the formal union of the two parties pointed to the disparity between them. He took the vestigial rump of the SDP into an unimaginatively titled 'Continuing Social Democratic Party', along with distinctively unfashionable policies such as monetarism and Euroscepticism. Meanwhile the new party settled down to a public unity and the development of a slow-burning internal trauma.

The Liberals

The Liberals and the Social Democrats are working within different discourses and by a different understanding of the purpose and potential of government. David Laws's opposition to the restoration of the pensions–earnings link and his support for private health insurance showed an appreciation of the benefits of non-state solutions for social problems that he feels fits snugly into the liberal tradition. In *The Orange Book* he wrote:

> The proposal [for a national insurance scheme] is essentially for a far reaching reform, which can be regarded as being similar to a system of competing social insurance schemes, with the existing NHS service representing one of the competing options [as well as the default option].
>
> Each scheme would levy the same maximum annual charge for membership, for a standard range of all mainstream clinical services. Additional charges could be paid by those people willing to pay for higher quality non-clinical services, such as private rooms. Such 'enhancement' charges would be set by each health insurance provider.

This scheme would introduce an unprecedented level of competition for the production of services in the NHS. It would radically alter the nature of healthcare provision, placing greater emphasis upon the role of the private sector and reducing the NHS to the part of a competing enterprise, an uncompetitive safety net for poorer consumers that would presumably eventually wither away. Arguably the option of 'opting out' of NHS provision represents a departure from the concept of 'free at the point of delivery', or at least a rewriting of it. Wealthy patients could buy themselves better treatment. It is a proposal that is remarkably close to the spirit of the reforms championed by the Soho right of the Conservative Party.

To Laws and the Liberals within his party, such a critical approach to the potential of the state to be a good provider is a badge of intellectual continuity with the past. Throughout the 2005 conference references were made to the philosophy of John Stuart Mill, citing the Victorian grandee as an example of a variety of a small-state liberalism that might appeal to the British middle classes. The flipside of utilitarianism, with its message of democratic civil co-operation, is the primacy of the individual and the desirability of limiting state interference. In the United States liberalism has faced little opposition from socialists enamoured of the state and too much from libertarians who fear it. As a result it has become defined mostly by its confidence in the abilities of government. In Great Britain this has not been the case. British Liberalism was raised between the Scylla of ultra-Toryism in the early nineteenth century, which opposed any involvement of the government in welfare provision at all, and the Charybdis of the Labour movement of the twentieth, with its economic interventionism. Many British Liberals accept the social contract and government involvement with regret, if not full-blown suspicion. Utilitarianism, the creed at the heart of the *Orange Book*, is often regarded as a recipe for the social contract. *On Liberty*, Mill's opus and the bible of modern liberalism, is read by some Liberal thinkers as an elegy for the death of the individual in the context of the rise of the state. It seeks to chart a course between the growth of government and the rights of man, not to enhance the collectivist project but explicitly to defend individual liberty as much as possible. 'The subject of this essay', writes Mill, '. . . is civil or social liberty: the nature and limits of the power which can legitimately be exercised by society over the individual . . . the struggle between liberty and authority'. Many of Mill's solutions are antecedents to policies proposed by Laws and the *Orange Book*. They have often been used to provide a good indicator of a liberal approach to public service and welfare provision.

Indeed, it is perfectly possible to skim Mill and find a quote to support such a thesis. For instance, in *On Liberty* he states:

> Though individuals may not do the particular thing [civil or industrial enterprise] well, on average as the officers of government, it is nevertheless desirable that a thing should be done by them, rather than by the government as a means to their own education. . . . This is a principal, though not the sole, recommendation of jury trial (in cases not political); of free and popular local municipal institutions; of the conduct of industrial and *philanthropic exercises by voluntary associations*. . . . Government operations tend to be everywhere alike.

> With individuals and voluntary associations on the contrary, there are varied
> experiments and an endless diversity of experience . . . [The state's] business is
> to enable each experimentalist to benefit by the experiments of others, instead
> of tolerating no experiments but its own. [emphasis added]

Apparently, Mill's object is both to preserve individual liberty and to erect a structure by which society might function in the best needs of the majority. This model would not only appreciate the capacity of voluntary or private organisations to carry out welfare provision but would in fact favour it. In this context it is easy to understand how a politician such as Laws could support private health insurance.

It is not of interest here to debate the value of evolving an approach to government based on the experience of the nineteenth century; indeed, one could praise the Liberals for trying to identify a raison d'être at all. But Laws's claim to intellectual consistency is not altogether solid. Mill is often appropriated by Liberal Democrats of either wing for the sake of claiming historical and philosophical coherence. As such, the regularity with which he is quoted is evidence of the uncertainty over how precisely he should be interpreted and the ease with which politicians with widely differing views group around him. During the 2006 leadership contest Chris Huhne would invoke his memory when arguing for a ban on smoking in public; Menzies Campbell would describe his influence upon him as 'indelible'; and, when elected president of the party in 2004, Simon Hughes proudly received a ceremonial copy of On Liberty. Mill is hard to pin down, but probably does not belong too firmly to the Liberal tradition of Laws and the party's right. He altered his views on the role of monopoly and the state at various points. For instance, in Book V of Principles of Political Economy he indicated that where monopoly would not be compulsory and the government agency could pay its own expenses, privatisation would not necessarily be a good thing. The utilitarian philosophy of Mill places greater emphasis upon flexibility within economics than do the modern Liberals. Indeed, he suggests that:

> There are other things, of the worth of which the demand of the market is by
> no means a test; things of which the utility does not consist in ministering to

inclinations, nor in serving the daily uses of life, and the want of which is least felt where the need is greatest.

Some have attributed to this scepticism of the benefits of the market a proto-socialism. This seemingly unimportant point is in fact quite vital. Contemporary Liberal thinking finds more in common with the works of Adam Smith. As such its glorification of laissez-faire economics belongs to the Liberal Party of the early nineteenth century, putting it at odds with the later Liberal tradition that favoured government intervention. It is with that later tradition that the Social Democrats tend to prefer to associate.

This association perhaps places too great a trust in the enthusiasm of later Liberal governments for welfarism and intervention, governments described by Hughes as having an 'agenda of social justice'. The orthodoxy of the nineteenth century was that free markets were both economically and ethically preferable to intervention, to the degree to which the government would intervene to protect them. On occasion this would result in war to expand markets, but most often it resulted in tentative steps towards a welfare system. The purpose of this was not to alter democratic capitalism but to refine it in order to make it more productive. This produced a generosity towards social reform within Liberal governments that was treated sceptically by some. As the indefatigable George Bernard Shaw put it, 'it became the custom for Liberal governments to give a minor ministerial post to some mild middle class professor who was vaguely supposed to be interested in factory legislation and popular education, and who was openly treated as a negligible nobody by the rest of the Cabinet.'

Towards the end of the nineteenth century, fear began to grow in Britain that it was being outpaced by Germany in industrial and military production, symbolised by the publication of E. E. Williams's *Made in Germany* in 1896, which warned of potential Prussian domination of Europe. This fear carried on into the twentieth century and at its height the Liberal Party formed a 'War Budget' in 1909, which would fight poverty by producing dreadnoughts, linking economic and military efficiency. David Lloyd George toured Germany and was mightily impressed by the impact upon production of raised living standards and by the fledgling union movement. Liberal social provision was thus written in the language of economic efficiency, not the welfarism of post-war Britain. A Liberal magazine, the *Speaker*, reiterated in 1905 that money spent on pensions would be saved on Poor Law expenditure and that healthier workers could labour a little longer.

If modern Liberal 'ideology' is rooted in an early nineteenth-century love of the market and misreading of Mill, then Social Democrats are equally mistaken to regard early twentieth-century Prime Ministers as their spiritual forefathers. Capitalism evolved through the 1800s to a point where it required state management of society to feed it. Thus British Liberalism has, like its American counterpart, always sought to manage the economy and society. In the case of the latter it even reformed the British constitution. For some Liberals this was an act of empowerment, but for many more it was a method of staving off revolution. In 1909 Winston Churchill, then a member of the Liberal government, reflecting upon his party's adoption of social reform, commented that 'workingmen's insurance' offered the poor 'a stake in the country [with which] these workers will pay no attention to the vague promises of revolutionary socialism'. When it came to granting women the right to vote, many within the Liberal Party felt their movement had overstretched itself. There is no doubt that the latter Liberal regimes had a more sophisticated understanding of the relationship between state and market, arguably an approach that put daylight between the movement in the early twentieth century and Smith and the modern Liberals. But it was still heavily influenced by the needs of production and whether or not this tradition rests easily with the party's Social Democrats, many of whom are essentially 'wet' socialists, remains to be seen.

Meanwhile the Liberals within their party are creatures of the even more distant past, their rhetoric suffused with the priorities of early nineteenth-century liberalism. Often this message is confused by a hijacking of the language New Labour uses to flag up its public-spending proposals. Edward Davey MP gave a speech in 2004 that proposed a Tory policy in Labour's language: 'At the next election Liberal Democrats will be the party of tax cuts. Tax cuts for the many, not the few.' The Liberals have not just promoted tax reforms that create a more equitable structure, such as their much-touted plan to abolish the current council tax system, but tax cuts and spending cuts have also been praised as good things in and of themselves. Vince Cable MP told an audience at the 2004 conference:

> Our approach to public spending is disciplined and starts from the simple point that for every new spending commitment there has to be an equivalent cut in public spending somewhere else.
>
> We will make the tax system fairer; less regressive. For the majority of voters the Lib Dems will mean tax cuts, not tax increases . . . I believe that in any debate, whether it is on the doorstep, in Parliament or through the media, our philosophy of a liberal and financially disciplined approach to economic problems with a social conscience will win through.

The stressing of fiscal discipline and the inherent benefits of tax reduction resemble closely the philosophy of Soho modernisers within the Conservative Party. The only difference is that it is untempered by social moralising. In many regards it is purely 'neo-libertarian', seeking to extract the state from people's lives as much as possible. As such it is Thatcherism without the fire and brimstone. Modern Liberals do not assume that a reduction in state interference will lead to stable families and clean living. They do not care whether it does or not.

But the devil is limited to the detail only; on the surface the Liberal Democrats continue to appear supportive of government intervention. Malcolm Bruce MP also spoke at the 2004 conference of his proposals to save the Post Office: 'Government policy has destroyed the viability of our post office network. Urban branches have been closed in their thousands. More than half of the rural network of over 9,000 offices is under threat. Once viable post office businesses are now unsellable.' By the very fact of talking about necessary government intervention one might be forgiven for thinking that he favoured nationalisation. The contrary was true. Bruce laid the blame firmly on government control:

> The thousands of businessmen and women who run the post offices are effectively subsidising the network. Unless lost income is replaced quickly we will lose the national network that Liberal Democrats across the country are

fighting to secure . . . We need a business plan to develop new services and co-ordinate government and other public and private information services through post offices.

The Liberal Democrats' 2005 policy document *Setting Business Free* called for the privatisation of the Post Office. This is a position either not popular with or else unknown to the party faithful. For instance, the MEP Baroness Ludford wrote to several local papers in the 2005 general election to register her complete opposition to post office closures and part privatisation. She preferred the solution of reducing internet sales to encourage a return to the use of the Royal Mail, a policy at odds with her party's demand in the business policy paper that 'technology must not and should not be stopped from yielding efficiency gains'. Liberal Democrat economic policy, apparently in the ascendance, is framed by its understanding of the laissez–faire traditions of Liberalism. As such it stands in contrast to the beliefs of those who have joined the party as a left-leaning alternative to Tony Blair or the inheritors of the social democratic tradition. This point cannot be made strongly enough. The Liberal Democrats do not in their economic policy favour a clear alternative to the embrace of the free market of New Labour and the Conservatives. Elements of their platform would challenge many of the precepts of the welfare state.

The British Liberal movement, now going through a quiet renaissance, has always rejected structural economic explanations of human behaviour and the necessity of regulation, reform or control of the free market. For instance, when the Liberal government of Lloyd George came to introduce the country's first ever old age pension, it omitted provision for those deemed by their communities to be low in personal morals or alcoholic. Because Liberals reject the view that people's behaviour is influenced by society or economics, they reasoned that Britain was divided between the deserving and the undeserving poor. Such a position rejects the notion that the poor are trapped by economic structures and as such does not seek to challenge it. To those on the left drifting towards the Liberal Democrats this should pose a fundamental question about the value of endorsing the third party. Indeed, the Liberals' cynicism towards the value of state intervention puts them on a collision course with the Social Democrats, who now make up an increasing share of the party's membership.

The Social Democrats

The origins and nature of Social Democratic thinking are without distinct clarity. Historians and protagonists still debate why the SDP split from the Labour Party, what the theoretical basis was for the creation of a new party and to whom they eventually appealed. This is in part a reflection of the disparity of the personalities involved. Bill Rodgers was a stolid man of the Labour right who had played a significant role in the nationalisation of the dockyards. David Owen was a dynamic supporter of the Common Market who later denounced his colleagues when he reversed his position to campaign against membership of the European Union, and, while leader of the SDP in the late 1980s, indicated that he would prefer to work in a Cabinet under Margaret Thatcher than Neil Kinnock. Shirley Williams was considerably to Owen's left on economic issues and as Secretary of State for Education had slaved through the late 1970s to abolish grammar schools. But the character most hard to pin down was that of Roy Jenkins, a socially reclusive man from a strong Labour and union background. In comparison with the others, he was described by Rodgers as being 'much less committed to an identifiable political philosophy'. Certainly in lectures and writing prior to forming the SDP, Jenkins stressed the need to reinvigorate the three-party system rather than the benefits of a new ideology, to overhaul 'the constricting rigidity – almost the tyranny of the three-party system'.[1]

There is a perfectly sound reason why a philosophical rationale is hard to find: one never existed. The foundation of the SDP was based on an immediate political decision, another example of historical accident creating its own deterministic future. That historical accident was the rise of the Bennite left. Some of the first members of the SDP left the Labour Party because they feared their careers would be endangered by its new radicalism. They suspected that they might be deselected by the leftists taking control of the constituency parties, as had happened to

Dick Taverne MP, who in the 1970s was forced to run as an independent and later joined the Conservatives. Even if they won reselection, the unpopularity of the hard left among the public might lose them their seats at the general election. But most quit the party not because they disagreed over materialism or even the tenets of socialism but because of individual policies that had briefly become causes célèbres. None of these policies was economic and as a result the SDP would enter the 1983 general election not promising a single privatisation. The policies over which they had resigned included disarmament and membership of the European Economic Community. But most potently, they quit over who controlled the policy-making process of the Labour Party. The SDP was founded to a large degree in response to alarm at growing thuggish behaviour at Labour conferences and the rise of the undemocratic 'democratic left'. The founders did not disagree with the values that the Labour Party had always expressed; they simply felt that the party could no longer sustain those values. In 1980 Williams, Owen and Rodgers, while still Labour members, wrote an open letter in which they warned that if their party 'abandons its democratic and internationalist principles, the argument may grow for a new democratic socialist party to establish itself as a party of conscience and reform committed to those principles'. Thus the SDP was formed not as a result of a liberal critique of Labour's traditional values, some-thing the Liberal Party would have naturally embraced, but in reaction to a set of short-term circumstances that drove moderate socialists out of their own party.

If historically the proof of the pudding has so often been in the eating, then the SDP tasted like low-calorie Labour. The Limehouse Declaration, the pronouncement of the formation of the new party and its core aims, reads in the context of New Labour like a copy of the *Socialist Worker*. It rejected the politics of triangulation and reaching to the centre for its own sake, 'representing the lowest common denominator between two extremes'. It strove for 'an open, classless and more equal society . . . to eliminate poverty, promote greater equality'. A flavourless cherry on the top told its readers that it supported 'more, not less radical change in our society, but with a greater stability of direction'. The ensuing alliance with the Liberals produced a manifesto in 1983 that does not sit comfortably with the fiscal conservatism and enthusiasm for private investment that is evident in the modern party. Some commentators have focused on the right-wing elements of the manifesto. This is wrong, as the policies over which the SDP split from their party of origin – unilateralism, immediate withdrawal from the EEC and drastic constitutional reform – were innovations for Labour too. To study those policy positions in isolation as evidence that the SDP was significantly to the right of the Labour movement is incorrect as it ignores the fact that the Labour Party had veered briefly to the far left on a number of emotional issues. A better evaluation of where the SDP sat in the socialist tradition can be garnered from its views on economics rather than on its disagreements with Tony Benn and the Militant Tendency. In 1983 it proposed to increase public borrowing to around £11 billion, exactly the same amount promised by the Labour Party's manifesto. An example of the alliance's Keynesianism and dedication to the preservation of the welfare state was given by its pledge on social services:

> There is a great need for extra support staff in the NHS and the personal social services. These services are highly labour-intensive and their greatest need for extra people is in regions of high unemployment. We propose the establishment of a special £500 million Fund for the health and social services in order to create an additional 100,000 jobs of this kind over two years.

It is true that this manifesto was written at a time of remarkably high unemployment, but this faith in the importance of deficit social spending earned Liberal Party leader David Steel opprobrium from within his own party for agreeing to it and even the threat of a leadership challenge. It was a reflection of an SDP-influenced enthusiasm for government intervention. The SDP of 1983 showed its roots when discussing industrial and economic policy. On the north/ south divide, it argued that conflict would be resolved 'not by intimidating the unions through unemployment. Not by nationalising, de-nationalising, re-nationalising.' Rather it would encourage an industrial democracy of the 1980s, share ownership and 'increased funding for the Co-operative Development Agency – to provide advice and financial support for those setting up co-operatives'. Again, the SDP's conflict with Labour's policies was not philosophical but political. It did not disapprove of nationalisation, but disagreed with the use of public industries to advance 'class warfare' or of direct government control in order to permit greater leniency in industrial dispute and greater financial gain for the Treasury:

> We must get away from the incessant and damaging warfare over the *ownership* of industry and switch the emphasis to how well it performs. Thus we will retain the present position of British Aerospace but will not privatise British Telecom's main network nor sell off British Airways. But we will make the nationalised industries successful and efficient as well as properly responsible to their consumers.

In essence the Labour Party's short-term political crisis of the early 1980s had created an uncomfortable alliance of Liberals and Social Democrats. Continuity of Social Democratic thinking in the modern Liberal Democratic Party is clear, as is its unavoidable conflict with Liberal economic thinking.

Many modern Liberal Democrat MPs, particularly those from outside the south-west, sport an agenda that is notably warm towards government intervention and increased public investment to a degree that places them at odds with Liberal fiscal discipline. An example is Simon Hughes MP, who, typically for a left-wing Liberal Democrat MP, represents an ex-Labour seat. In a 2006 interview he admitted that his image was not immediately appealing to Conservatives: 'I come from a tradition that is more compatible with Labour – the redistribution of wealth and a fairer society.' Speaking in Parliament in 2005 on the subject of housing benefit, he asked:

> Will the government please back off from insisting . . . that everything that is efficient must be done outside the public sector and that everything that is inefficient is inefficient because of the public sector? When Southwark ran these matters itself, it did so very well; when these matters were contracted out, they were handled badly. There is a moral there somewhere, which might be that we should sometimes let councils get on with the job themselves and not force them

always to contract out . . . Can we please take the pressure off and allow local authorities to make the choices that they think are best, rather than forcing them to contract everything out into the private sector because of a dogmatic view in central government?

During his leadership bid, Hughes redirected that attack to the Liberals within his own party, stating, 'They assume you have to apply free market principles to everything . . . I don't accept that.' It is possible to argue that Hughes was reflecting not an ideological commitment to public ownership but instead a 'solutions-based' approach to government that supported private management where possible and government intervention where necessary. It is impossible to read one man's soul or that of the entire Liberal Democrat back benches and it should be noted that Hughes has opposed every act of privatisation passing through Parliament since being elected to it, but that his is not a totally socialist doctrine is unimportant. What is vital is that his appreciation of the capacity of government to manage the economy and public-service provision is high enough to set him at loggerheads with the Liberals within his party. Indeed, although Hughes may not have an ideological commitment to enhancing and enlarging the public sphere, his colleagues from the West Country and the Liberal tradition do have an ideological commitment to shrinking it.

Prospects

It is instructive to reiterate that the only policy areas in the 2005 general election in which the Liberal Democrats enjoyed popularity amongst the British public were Iraq and the environment. The first does not offer a long-term electoral strategy for third-party politics. Given the contentious nature of the war, it had the capacity to cross party boundaries and attract to the Liberal Democrats a wide field of voters, but it is unlikely to be a doorstep issue in four or five years' time. Interestingly, at face value the second policy area does hold immense promise. Environmentalism is a tempting flagship policy for a third party, evidenced in part by David Cameron's adoption of it within days of his leadership victory. It became a familiar theme in the Liberal Democrats' own contest. Menzies Campbell told an interviewer in the first week that his three priorities were 'the environment, the environment, the environment'. More strikingly, Chris Huhne, who openly sought comparison with Cameron by reminding journalists that 'it seems to be the year for outsiders', chose it as his campaign's sole theme. He accepted the prevailing view that it was necessary to squeeze philosophical debate from the campaign and to avoid associating the party with ideology of any variety. 'We need', he told a London audience, 'to unite around a policy programme that combines all of the goals that our consciences crave with the pragmatic solutions that our heads can devise. This is not left nor right. Not *Orange Book* versus *Yellow Book*. Not social liberalism versus economic liberalism.' Environmentalism was Huhne's preferred cause. His declaration speech made it clear that it was his priority. Subsequent speeches and articles typically lambasted the Labour and Tory records ('Labour's deeds in office have not matched its green words' and 'The Conservatives are about as green as an oil slick') followed by a series of suggestions for green taxes and tougher targets. Overall Huhne's campaign escaped clear ideological definition, inviting comparison with that of Liam Fox. One *Times* commentator dubbed him 'to the left' while a *Telegraph* writer felt his chances were hurt by being perceived as 'right wing'. This was partly because he made an effort to appeal to as broad a range of activists as possible, which he achieved more by what he neglected to talk about, than what he did talk about. Huhne has spent six years in the European Parliament and as a devotee of further integration one might expect him to have discussed his considerable experience in his campaign. He did not.

Rather, he decided to focus upon environmentalism. This was strategically sensible, as it is decidedly inoffensive and arguably the perfect issue for a party that is the product of the dash to the centre ground to focus on. Although recession has made it a controversial topic in the United States, in Britain a rising quality of life has given environmentalism appeal that reaches across generations, class, party affiliation and region. To the wet Tory in the south-east it translates in to conservation, specifically protecting the green belt. To the south-western or Scottish Liberal it is the protection of habitats, fish stocks and holding the line against the sludge of industrialism. To the London left-wing activist it is bicycle lanes and taking on the corporations. As a tactic in a leadership election highlighting green issues garnered Huhne significant attention, but it poses several hidden problems for the national party. It is symptomatic of how triangulation can damage even those parties that seem to benefit most from it, forcing them to eschew philosophical debate in return for focusing on inoffensive policies that polls imply offer only limited electoral reward. The Liberal Democrats may avoid confrontation by avoiding open internal debate on education, health and the economy, but they risk association with purely fringe or temporary issues. They could become like the European Green parties, admittedly enjoying reasonable election results but with no hope of forming a government in their own right. Moreover in the scramble for the centre, the parties of the 'Ancien Régime' have got wise, the Conservatives trying to seize the green mantle in an aggressive act of triangulation that might actually force the Liberal Democrats clearly to the Tories' left. Huhne's candidacy teetered on single-issue politics, and it would be foolish for the Liberal Democrats as a whole to follow suit.

Environmentalism may well represent a genuine passion and commitment, but it also threatens to be a cover for the intense division between liberalism and social democracy. Its predominance was symptomatic of a leadership battle that desperately tried to avoid debating principles. In so doing it did not unite the party, nor secure a happy or commanding future for either faction. For the Liberals the problem remains that their erstwhile comrades in the wider party are in the ascendancy. There is a public perception that the Liberal Democrats have moved to the left, and the Liberals in the party have lost seats as a result. In 2005 they lost five broadly middle-class seats to the Tories – Torridge & West Devon, Guildford, Ludlow, Newbury and Weston-super-Mare – when they had hoped to gain some. These losses suggest a decline in the constituency of disaffected Conservative voters, which may well strengthen the Social Democrats' hand, both in terms of their role in the formation of policy and in their proportion of seats in

Parliament. Public attention has been focused on Liberal Democrat gains from Labour for purely mathematical reasons. After the 1997 and 2001 results, there appeared to be more Labour seats to target than Conservative ones. But once more this was a false perception on the part of the public; Conservative marginals have always been and remain the Liberal Democrats' only hope of breaking into triple figures in terms of parliamentary seats. The party has flagged up the issues on which it differs from Labour and the Tories in a way that has presented it as left wing, arguably to the detriment of winning over Tory voters. As we saw above, in 2005 the public rated the Liberal Democrats as preferable to the other two parties only on the policy areas of Iraq and the environment. This would imply that the message of fiscal discipline is either unpopular or not being communicated. Certainly media attention was focused more upon Liberal Democrat foreign policy in 2005 than its economic thinking. Also the areas of policy upon which there is undoubted convergence between Social Democrats and Liberals, particularly civil liberties and law and order, rarely attract Conservative support. Opposition to ID cards, liberalisation of drug laws and lowering the legal drinking age to sixteen are bread and water to Social Democrats and wandering Labour supporters, but not the Conservatives with whom the Liberals would prefer to bolster the party's ranks. If David Cameron succeeds in making his party at least appear competent then it can be assumed that 'wet' Tories will return to the fold, rather than stay with a party that sees its future as lying to the left of Labour.

After the general election Lord Rennard, who drew up the Liberal Democrats' list of target seats, and Lord Razzall, who chaired the campaign and directed its strategy, became the subject of unprecedented private criticism. They were accused of failing to deliver messages that appealed simultaneously to Labour and Tory voters and of failing to neutralise a growing appearance of drifting to the left. Moreover, the contentious nature of much policy passed at Conference attests to an influx of left-leaning activists into the party. Increasingly the Liberal Democrats will find it difficult to maintain their image of being above ideology and free from the right–left discourse when their party is monopolised by those keen to oppose Labour's agenda of privatisation, rather than to balance budgets and deregulate the economy. The 2006 leadership election has left it almost impossible to avoid association with ideology altogether.

The burning question remains as to what future there is for the Liberal Democrats as the new dominant party of the British left. There are problems too for the Social Democrats. Few of their MPs are from the Liberal Democrat heartland of the south-west and if the movement declines in votes at the next election they will be the first to lose their seats. At present their social values are well expressed within party policy, but on economics they remain at odds with much of the parliamentary membership. In fact there is a viable comparison with the state of the Labour Party in the early 1980s. The radical activists are not adequately represented in their views by the front bench, yet enjoy a flexible degree of power at Conference and in the shires, possibly giving rise to conflict. The influence of MPs such as Vince Cable and David Laws on economic policy could cause a long-term battle over interpretations of state power and responsibility. Some Social Democrats have already shown evidence of frustration. Paul Marsden, the MP who defected to the Liberal Democrats over the war, returned shortly before the election. Camden councillor Jonathan Simpson – former Liberal Democrat parliamentary candidate for Hampstead & Highgate, Liberal Democrat candidate in 2004 for the Barnet & Camden constituency in the London Assembly and former Liberal Democrat group whip in Camden – also defected in 2005. He explained that he was

> increasingly disillusioned with the effectiveness and seriousness of the Lib Dems for some time and that has become more evident since I was elected as a councillor. In terms of policies Labour has shown the lead in many areas with the Lib Dems floundering. The Lib Dems' stance on crime and anti-social behaviour is weak and on the economy, I was very disappointed with their opposition to the minimum wage.

But even if the Social Democrats were to dominate all areas of the manifesto, there is no evidence that they could replace the Labour Party as the major party of the left. Historical experience certainly casts doubt upon such a seismic shift taking place. Throughout the 1920s and 1930s, the Liberal Party was Britain's only Keynesian party. Under Ramsay MacDonald and Philip Snowden the Labour Party fought for social reform, but eschewed government intervention in the economy. Ironically, the Liberals embraced it, arguing for deficit-funded programmes of public works. Nevertheless the policy failed in its objective to win over working-class support. The Liberal Democrats simply do not have the necessary structures of influence over what remains of the Labour movement and its coalition. It does not have the symbiotic relationship with the unions necessary to generate influence over the working classes or to give it credibility among them. Although triangulation has undermined Labour's coalition, it would take a Herculean effort to replace it totally, as some Social Democrats seem to wish to do. Such an effort would require a precipitous shift in the political and social makeup of the party, to such a degree that conflict with its Liberal membership and a resultant implosion would be inevitable. Moreover if, or when, Gordon Brown assumes the Labour leadership, then many left-wing voters may feel either culturally attracted back to their old party or motivated to support it by a potential general election tie with the Conservatives. A competent Tory Party and a Labour Party facing defeat may act as a pincer movement on the Liberal Democrat vote.

Charles Kennedy's resignation and the 2006 leadership race prove that it is no exaggeration to state that the Liberal Democrats are capable of civil war. In 2004 one letter from a member of the party's national executive to the *Guardian* asked of the authors of the *Orange Book*:

> Why are they so determined to start a punch up between nineteenth-century classical liberals and twentieth-century social liberals? Surely the task in the twenty-first century is to reforge liberalism for a new era, which looks set to be marked by struggles over increasingly limited natural resources, a rapidly expanding global population and the effects of climate change? Pretending that John Stuart Mill, Gladstone or Beveridge have all the answers is the height of folly.

In terms of political evolution, the Liberal Democrats are not as suited to long-term survival as their success in 2005 indicates. Rather, their adaptation to the New Politics is only successful in part and that which they have achieved could later prove self-harming. It is true that the decline in traditional voting patterns has permitted them to garner many more votes than they ever have done before. But it has not awarded them a coherent electorate and one of the requisite size to form an opposition, let alone a government. This is because the Liberal Democrats are as much a prisoner of the past as their opponents are. That they are the current beneficiaries of triangulation is sheer happy accident. They represent two distinctly different moulds of political thought, one with its roots in the nineteenth century and one with its identity formed by the breakup of the democratic left at the end of the 1970s. The latter, the Social Democratic wing, was created out of short-term political circumstance and did not represent a coherent divorce from the philosophy of the Labour movement. Its alliance with the Liberals was also the product of the peculiar circumstances of the early 1980s. The formal union of the two towards the end of the decade was actually a recognition that the alliance, or at least the Social Democratic wing of it, had all but electorally died. Since 2001 it has gained steam because Labour and the Conservatives have lost it under the weight of triangulation. Large numbers of people voted Liberal Democrat unenthusiastically, with little knowledge of its policies and with no understanding at all of the cultural history behind their party of new-found indulgence. It is true that the Liberal Democrats have proved capable of building short-term coalitions among different interest groups. The combination of Asian and student voters toppled Labour in a number of seats, although it is important to stress once more that this was evidence of sectional response to individual policy errors made by the government. But these partnerships in opposition are not enough to form a government. Moreover the very process of forming such coalitions is likely to alienate a whole swathe of moderate Conservative voters that a centrist party would need to form a government. The evidence from the 2005 general election returns is that this process has already begun.

The first half of this book castigated the two main parties for failing to adapt to the New Politics of the post-Cold War era. In the process of abandoning coherent concepts and discourse of 'why we choose to govern' they have shed their electorates. The rise of the Liberal Democrats is proof that this process is taking place, but it is far from being its ultimate outcome. The Liberal Democrats share all of their opponents' flabby flaws. Whilst weighed down with internal and vibrant divisions which they currently do not boast the structure to resolve, they have failed to put forward a coherent alternative proposal for how Britain should be governed. Indeed the very concept of a Liberal–Social Democratic alliance is simply unrealistic. One side proposes a morality-lite variant of the Soho Conservatives, while the other provides an economically socialistic movement grounded in the language of the early 1980s. The result has been a haphazard and lucky triangulation, one that has benefited from the present unpopularity of the two-party system. While this has allowed the Liberal Democrats to win the greatest number of seats since its foundation, the edifice of their success has been erected on shifting sands. Lacking a coherent and consistent programme with which to fight future elections, the Liberal Democrats necessarily depend on triangulation, making them into a party of protest that is subject to the readjustment of the other parties' fortunes. As the centre ground is realigned, and as the Conservatives' own process of triangulation leaves them better prepared to compete for this political territory, the Liberal Democrats' electoral assets seem likely to evaporate. Given the foundations on which they have built their present success and the likely causes of their future demise, the Liberal Democrats appear as the best illustration of the effects of the New Politics on British political discourse. Their recent history is the ultimate expression of the failure of triangulation to construct coherent philosophies, national identities and clear political purpose. That these things are hungrily and increasingly sought outside the traditional political establishment altogether is the concern of the next chapter. But for this one, the only conclusion that can be reached is that the Liberal Democrats are not the solution to our modern political malaise. They are symptomatic of its very condition.

5

Minor parties, independents and the problem of pluralism

If a general election is a drama of one quality or another, minor political parties and independent candidates are apt to appear as the lesser characters of the play. They emerge on the stage only briefly; they may receive cheers, laughter or rancour; and once they have made their inglorious exit, they are forgotten until the production is revived a few years later. Some candidates, such as the leading lights of the Vote for Yourself Rainbow Dream Ticket Party, appear to have an even more tenuous relation to the central dialogue of political theatre. Candidates of this variety have occasion on the podium of the count to seem itinerant pantomime characters that, standing alongside more serious and dour actors, appear to be looking, Pirandello-like, for a suitable farce in which to feature.

Yet these lesser characters are not to be dismissed as unimportant. As with theatre, it is sometimes the actors that at first appear to demand the least attention who are later revealed to play a telling role in the unfolding of the drama. The tardy messenger of *King Lear* is a pertinent reminder of this. Similarly, it is often the case that the most incidental and even grotesque character reflects the central thrust of the whole production most clearly. The cackling clown in the background is perhaps occasionally the most exact reflection of the failures, flaws and future of more obvious players and, on rare occasions, even of the audience itself.

Examining minor political parties and independent candidates, therefore, is not simply a matter of exploring their own restricted fortunes in British elections. Nor should it be concerned merely with a consideration of their future prospects. There is no doubt that each of these perspectives is important, but their relevance to wider political issues is more significant. The British National Party, for example, is interesting to study, but studying it in isolation is rather like trying to gain an appreciation of the characters of Shylock, Othello or Malvolio by looking only at their soliloquies. Their role in the wider whole lies unexamined and no new insights into the political play are permitted. To take another example, the Green Party's performance at the polls may stimulate the curiosity in itself, but taken out of a broader political context, it is mere trivia. Combined with a close analysis of the political and sociological reasons for electoral shifts, however, the electoral fate of such minor parties can throw a powerful light on the wider political stage and illuminate the behaviour of the major characters more clearly.

Previous chapters have shown how the historical accident of Labour's managerial approach to government both connected with the recent collapse of its social constituency and also led to a general dearth of ideology in mainstream politics. The ramifications of this historical phenomenon for the internal politics and future direction of Labour, the Conservatives and the Liberal Democrats have been examined in depth. What remains unaddressed, however, is the broader impact of managerial politics and the strategy of triangulation on the British public. The demise of ideological dialogue in the years following Tony Blair's 1997 election victory is evidenced most emphatically by the disappearance of thought on the function of government and the confusion that has recently arisen on this subject. The impact this has had on the composition, behaviour and political attitudes of the population as a whole has great relevance for the future of each of the political parties but is nevertheless relatively hard to gauge except through an examination of what might be termed the margins. It is the explanation of the fortunes of the minor political parties and independent candidates which is of most use in directly revealing voters' perceptions of politics and, most pertinently, of government and state. These 'marginal' cases allow us to appreciate the full influence of New Labour's managerial rule on the topography of the political landscape and the immense need for ideological innovation in specific areas of British political thought.

Beyond the Greens: the rise and rise of minority candidates

In the runup to the 2005 election, minor parties and independents gained relatively little coverage in newspapers and practically no attention in television news bulletins. Labour, the Conservatives and the Liberal Democrats quite naturally dominated the media limelight. Where column inches were dedicated to treatment of the outside runners, however, a clear journalistic approach was followed that was perhaps based on an expectation of readers' interests. The critical, intelligent and searching dissection of policies that characterised so much of the treatment of Labour and the Conservatives was utterly absent from the brief articles dedicated to the minor parties. In its place was an obsession with personality. George Galloway, founder and leader of Respect: The Unity Coalition, was written of as a bold, quixotic and unpredictable character; his party, with its extraordinary commitment to a form of communitarian socialism that had last been seen immediately before the 1983 election, was simply not mentioned. More words were written about the status of Robert Kilroy-Silk's suntan than about Veritas's curious programme. Only the Greens were spoken of as a party per se, but even then in a cursory manner which itself owed more to their strategy of adopting a joint leadership than to the policies they were actually propounding. By contrast, the other minor parties were brushed aside: the BNP was ignored, the UK Independence Party (UKIP) was dismissed and those independents who had not taken the precaution of changing their names to a slogan or who had not lost a family member in Iraq were not examined.

Once the election was over, the pattern of coverage was rarefied and repeated. After his victory in Bethnal Green & Bow, Galloway was cautiously trumpeted, but treated with suspicion. The Greens were hailed as having enjoyed a great success across the country and subtly congratulated on being able to look forward to a seat in Parliament in the near future. Kilroy-Silk, having lost, was quietly forgotten and allowed to wander off to bask again in the sunset. With the solitary exception of Reg Keys, who had stood against Blair in Sedgefield, no other candidate or minor party received significant media attention.

The impression presented by the media of the performance of the minor parties and independents at the 2005 election was, however, misleading. While accurate in relating some elements of their performances, newspaper, radio and television reports omitted many of the most significant features. It was, for example, perfectly true that the Green Party had recorded some impressive results, putting it in a different and more promising political situation. Across England the party received over a quarter of a million votes and in Brighton Pavilion managed to beat the Liberal Democrats to third place, with 22 per cent of the vote. Elsewhere in the country, their performance was equally noteworthy. In Lewisham Deptford the party gained 4.6 per cent of the share of the vote relative to 2001 and held a respectable 11.1 per cent in total. Similarly, in Hackney South & Shoreditch they attracted 5.5 per cent more of the vote than at the previous general election and cut similar new ground in Battersea, Birmingham Edgbaston, Ealing Acton & Shepherd's Bush, Erith & Thamesmead and Warwick & Leamington, to name only a few. Their candidates were attracting an increasing level of support and the issues on which the party campaigned most strongly received more attention from the public at large. These successes were not merely a reflection of a more general trend among the minor parties but were in fact rather incidental when compared to those of others. In many cases UKIP, Veritas, Respect and the BNP thrived rather better than their environmentally inclined compatriots. Despite gaining only a very small proportion of the vote in most constituencies, UKIP won more than twice as many votes as the Greens in England (592,417 compared to 251,051). Similarly, in some regions Veritas succeeded in accumulating a larger aggregate share of the vote than the Greens, despite frequently lagging behind in specific constituencies. Although they gained rather fewer votes, however, the BNP and Respect deserve far more attention than either the Greens or their rivals in UKIP and Veritas.

Far from being a one-man sideshow, as the media were wont to present it, Respect actually fielded a number of candidates across the country, who fought their campaigns hard on very low budgets and with the millstone of voter ignorance hanging around their necks. Bearing the obstacles they had to face, the performance of some candidates appears extremely impressive, especially when compared to the Greens. Across England, they won almost 70,000 votes, which, although less than a third of the support that the Green Party won, was more highly concentrated. Their twenty-six candidates took an average of 6.8 per cent of the vote in the constituencies they contested, more than twice the average share achieved by UKIP candidates and double the average share achieved by those standing for the Green Party. In Tottenham and Leicester South Respect emerged from the polls with 6.4 per cent of the vote, but in Poplar & Canning Town their representative, Oliur Rahman, seized 16.8 per cent. In West Ham, Lindsey German took 19.5 per cent and came in second place; in East Ham, Abdul Khaliq Mian won 20.7 per cent, again coming second, and in Birmingham Sparkbrook, Salma Yaqoob took a staggering 27.5 per cent, only just behind the successful Labour candidate, Roger Godsiff (who was returned with an 8.6 per cent majority, having lost 21.4 per cent of the share of the vote since 2001), and well ahead of both the Conservatives and the Liberal Democrats. Hence, while Respect may not have won quite as many votes as other minor parties, its performance per candidate was far more remarkable and its success – in terms of providing a serious challenge to incumbents from the major parties – was much more impressive. Indeed, so striking was its appearance on the national political stage that Professor John Curtice, the deputy director of the Centre for Research into Elections and Social Trends, described it as 'easily the best performance by a far-left party in British electoral history'.

The BNP did not achieve any singular results as dazzling as that of Galloway's Respect, but the general picture of their performance is equally, if not more, impressive and similarly stands in stark contrast to the modest, but more widely reported, gains of the Greens. Again, their aggregate total was far less than that of other minor parties, gaining as they did only 189,570 votes throughout England, but the smaller number of candidates that they fielded had the effect of concentrating support in well-targeted areas. With fewer candidates, a lower aggregate number of votes could have a more significant and impressive effect on the political balance in the constituencies which were targeted. Throughout the north of England and the Midlands, the overwhelming majority of BNP candidates garnered between 4 and 9.5 per cent more of the vote than in 2001. On average, each of its candidates polled 4.3 per cent of the vote, an increase on the previous election's figure despite the party having fielded far more candidates in 2005. In Dewsbury their candidate gained an extra 8.6 per cent of the vote, pushing the party's overall share up to 13.1 per cent. In Barking the party increased its support by such a margin that it held no less than 16.9 per cent of the vote, putting their candidate, Richard Barnbrook, into third place, only twenty-seven votes behind his Conservative rival. An increasingly effective party machine, orchestrated by the shrewd, if forbidding, Nick Griffin, has been able to move the party away from its roots in the thoroughly thuggish National Front to the point where it is not only an established part of mainstream British politics but a major player in political debate in a large number of constituencies. Although the Greens won over 60,000 more votes across England, the BNP was able at the 2005 election to position itself to have a greater impact on politics by targeting seats selectively and successfully.

In a similar vein, there may have been few independent candidates who were as memorable as Reg Keys – and there were none who gave such a dignified and moving speech at a count – but there were many who achieved an equal and greater level of success. Several individuals standing on a highly localised platform managed to attract enough support to keep their deposits and hence to have a noticeable impact on the political balance in particular constituencies. Roy Atkins, standing as an independent in Ashfield, won 2,292 votes (5.5 per cent) and Dave Nellist, who styled himself the 'Socialist Alternative', won 1,874 votes (5.0 per cent) in Coventry North East. These two examples are reflective of a general pattern: across England, people concerned with highly specific local or political issues were able not merely to stand as serious candidates but also to garner enough support to acquit themselves credibly and to attract attention to their concerns. Many were sufficiently credible, in fact, that they were able to threaten the position of some candidates from major political parties. In Morley & Rothwell, for example, Robert Finnigan was able with 10.8 per cent of the vote (4,608 votes) to put serious pressure on the Liberal Democrats, despite the small increase they themselves achieved. More impressively, Harry

Brooks, standing as an independent in the Labour seat of Burnley, gained 14.8 per cent of the vote and pushed the Conservative candidate into fourth place. Indeed, Brooks could well be credited with preventing the capture of the seat by the Liberal Democrats: the Labour majority was, by coincidence, exactly 14.8 per cent.

More significant than any other independent candidature, however, was the remarkable re-election of Dr Richard Taylor as MP for Wyre Forest. A GP distressed by the state of healthcare in his constituency, Taylor won his seat for the first time in 2001 under the banner of Independent Kidderminster Hospital and Health Concern (IKHHC). Despite losing the support of 18.2 per cent of voters, however, he was able to retain a majority of just over 5,000 in May 2005. Unlike the only other elected independent candidate – Peter Law, a former Labour member of the Welsh Assembly who had broken with his party in Blaenau Gwent in protest at an all-women shortlist imposed during the selection process – Taylor stood on the basis of a purely local issue and had no established connections with any other political party. Unlike that of Law, therefore, his victory was a clear example of an independent candidate achieving a level of success which was sufficient to alter the nature of political dialogue in that region and which was more than adequate to put the performance of the Green Party into a more appropriate perspective.

The Greens' fortunes at the 2005 election were in themselves impressive, and the candidacies of George Galloway and Robert Kilroy-Silk were intriguing, but they were merely an indication of a much larger trend in British politics. It was not merely that the Green Party was winning greater support than at previous general elections, nor that a very left-wing anti-war party candidate had won a seat from a prominent Labour MP, but that minor parties and independent candidates were all gaining more votes. This trend, however, is even more striking when considered in a broader historical context. It is, in fact, possible to go further than the picture presented hitherto and to show that, far from being unusually successful for independents and minority parties, the 2005 general election was the culmination of a long period of growth experienced by all political activists outside the three major parties.

Despite the image presented by newspapers and television journalists, the success of minor parties and independent candidates at the 2005 election was, in fact, merely the latest manifestation of a renaissance in minor-party fortunes that has been going on since 1997. Those parties which have existed continuously since the fall of John Major's government have all succeeded in dramatically increasing their support at national polls. In 1997, the BNP won just under 36,000 votes at the general election. By 2001 this had grown to 47,000 and by 2005 to nearly 200,000 votes across the United Kingdom. UKIP, similarly, won almost 106,000 votes in 1997, and captured nearly half a million more votes in the 2005 election. Although the Green Party's fortunes collapsed at the 1997 election, they managed steadily to recoup their position and were able in 2005 to almost triple their support since Tony Blair's first election victory.

A parallel to this trend is provided by the increased numbers of parties and independent candidates standing at general elections since 1997. Although there are a large number of individuals whose candidature at various elections has been based on a platform that is undoubtedly ludicrous — such as the Death, Dungeons and Taxes Party and the Church of the Militant Elvis Party — there has been an exponential rise in the number of parties standing on a very serious ticket. The English Parliamentary Party, Families First, the Wessex Regionalists and the Croydon Pensions Alliance, although apparently extremely restricted in their political purview, were, along with Respect, some of more than a hundred minor parties that stood at the 2005 election, almost double the number that fielded candidates at the 2001 election.[1] Similarly, 137 candidates describing themselves as 'Independents' stood in 2001, but by 2005, this number had grown to 176. This massive increase is significant in two respects. In the first place, it indicates that there are more people and more groups willing to risk losing a £500 deposit for the sake of opposing major political parties in an election. In the second place, it demonstrates that there is sufficient electoral flexibility to allow for a greater number of minor parties and independent candidates. Unless there was the possibility of gaining a credible level of support, there would simply be no point in standing at all.

In fact, at the same time as the rise in minor and independent candidatures, there has been a massive surge in support for these political alternatives considered together. In 1992, barely 500,000 people voted for minor or independent candidates in constituencies across Britain. By 1997, this figure had almost tripled to 1,458,215 votes and accounted for 4.67 per cent of all votes cast. With the demise of the Referendum Party (which won 811,849 votes at the 1997 general election) after the death of Sir James Goldsmith, the figure dropped to 1,065,651 votes at the 2001 general election, but, with a lower turnout, still accounted for 4.04 per cent of votes cast. By 2005, however, more than 1.5 million people voted for minor and independent candidates. Not merely was this an appreciably larger figure than that which had been registered in 1997, but it also represented a far higher proportion of the total number of votes cast across the country (5.77 per cent). It is therefore clear that while specific minor parties – such as the BNP and UKIP – have experienced a renaissance in the years since 1997, this is only a part of a much bigger alteration in patterns of political activism and support in Britain. Not only have more political alternatives to the programmes of major parties been propounded in recent years, but these alternatives have collectively attracted a large and growing level of support around the country. In determining their political allegiance, more people who are politically interested enough to continue voting in an age of growing apathy are looking outside the confines of mainstream dialogue. Minority parties, single-issue candidates and independents are perceived with increasing frequency to represent the beliefs and aspirations of ordinary voters better than New Labour, the Conservatives or the Liberal Democrats.

There is no doubt that this phenomenon – so poorly observed by the British media in the aftermath of the 2005 election – is the counterpart of the development of a more volatile electorate described in Chapter 1. Yet its most fascinating dimension does not lie in the mere fact of its existence but resides in the reasons for its occurrence. Having traced the emergence of the strategy of triangulation, a managerial approach to government and the demise of ideological thinking in the years since 1997, it is more than interesting to query exactly why more and more voters are turning at elections to candidates who do not belong to any major political party. To establish this point is to determine precisely what is driving the increasing volatility of the electorate, to understand the socio-political effects of the collapse of ideology and to comprehend more clearly the key weaknesses of the terms of British political dialogue.

The 'no party' phenomenon and the protest model of voting

An obvious, even instinctive, explanation of the increasing success of minority parties and candidates at general elections is the growth in dissatisfaction with the three major political parties. As less faith is put in the policies and personalities of Labour, the Conservatives and the Liberal Democrats, more individual voters are inclined to register their protest by voting for alternative candidates, knowing that their chances of contributing to the election of an outside figure are minimal.

This explanation – which could conveniently be labelled the 'protest model' of minority support – has a considerable amount of evidence to recommend it. Most strikingly, a general disenchantment with major political parties has transformed with growing frequency into a form of negative voting. As voters have broadly felt themselves unable to associate readily with Labour, the Conservatives or the Liberal Democrats, it is not that they have necessarily decided to vote *for* any party outside the framework of conventional dialogue but that they have determined to vote *against* the major parties, considered collectively representative of the state of politics as a whole.

Polls conducted by MORI and ICM between 1997 and 2005 have illustrated very clearly that an increasing number of voters believe there is little difference between the three major parties. At the same time, companion polls have demonstrated a mounting dissatisfaction with the approach not only of the government but also of the Conservatives and the Liberal Democrats. In many key policy areas the number of people replying that they did not know which party had the best programme or that they thought none of the major parties had any good ideas at all has risen steadily since the election of New Labour. At the height of the Conservative government's unpopularity, in late March 1996, 22 per cent of people who believed that healthcare provision was an important issue said that they were unable to say that any of the major parties had 'the best policy'. This had risen to 36 per cent by late January 2000 and to 41 per cent by September 2004. Similarly, in April 1997 29 per cent of people who believed pensions were a key policy issue declined to give their support to any of the three main parties. By July 2000 this had grown to 45 per cent and by February 2005 to 49 per cent. The same picture was repeated in the overwhelming majority of policy areas.

Indeed, many polls demonstrated that there was not merely a rise in disaffection for particular parties and policies but also the development of a mounting distaste for mainstream political dialogue. This process has been observable since 1997, but it accelerated rapidly with the advent of very public and very particular failures which touched the entire edifice of parliamentary politics. Andrew Rawnsley's book *Servants of the People* impressively traced the decline in confidence in politicians' credibility that accompanied the scandals of New Labour's first term in office. Yet since then, confidence in the probity of all politicians has plummeted further. The Hutton inquiry that followed the death of government weapons expert David Kelly and the handling of the decision to go to war in Iraq were particularly important in diminishing public faith in parliamentary politics. An ICM poll for the *Guardian* following the publication of Lord Hutton's report showed that 90 per cent of people questioned did not in general trust the government to tell the truth. Another from March 2004, which asked individuals about the war in Iraq, showed that 70 per cent of voters did not believe the government had been truthful in its handling of the war. The effect of this on public perceptions of the major parties and their leaders is easy to see. By July 2005 MORI found that none of Tony Blair, Michael Howard and Charles Kennedy were believed to be doing a satisfactory job as leader of their party by a majority of voters. Three months earlier, in the leadup to the general election, Robert Worcester reported that 53 per cent of voters could not say that Kennedy was trustworthy, 69 per cent replied that they couldn't believe Blair and fully 73 per cent declined to give credence to Howard. At the same time as the electorate was withdrawing its approval for any of the major political parties in specific policy areas, it is more than evident that its faith in parliamentary politics and mainstream politicians generally plummeted.

The growth of what has become known as the 'No Party' phenomenon is a powerful indication of the dislocation many voters have felt with the programmes propounded by Labour, the Conservatives and the Liberal Democrats. It is, furthermore, stark evidence that dissatisfaction has developed from the specific policy outcomes of the practices of the New Politics. Under these conditions of discontent, supporting political alternatives – in the shape of minority candidates – is a way of maintaining a level of engagement with the political process while still registering protest at the failures of the major parties. Unable to give their vote to any one of the Conservatives, Labour or the Liberal Democrats, electors turn to a party about whose policies they know little, but who are neither actively abhorrent nor likely actually to win a seat in Parliament. An example of this was readily observable in Cambridge in the weeks immediately prior to the 2005 election. All of the candidates standing were interviewed by a local newspaper and were each asked which party they would support if they could not vote for their own. With only one exception apart from the Green candidate himself, all of those who named another party named the Green Party. It was not that any of the candidates actually supported the Greens. Far from it: very few had any sympathy with the radically left-wing social and economic implications of some of the party's policies. Rather, the candidates who named the Greens simply didn't want to support any of their other rivals and saw the Green Party as the least obnoxious opportunity for protest.

Some candidates actively campaigned on the basis of appealing to the 'protest vote' impulse. Peter Law, although a Labour Party man at heart, was successful in defeating the official Labour candidate in Blaenau Gwent because of his ability to portray himself as a 'protest candidate'. In a *Newsnight* interview immediately following the announcement of his election to Westminster, Law repeatedly stressed his belief that his victory would 'send a message' to Blair, despite the fact that he guardedly conceded that in Parliament he would be likely to accept the Labour whip. Reg Keys, who stood against the Prime Minister in Sedgefield, having lost his son in Iraq, was another, perhaps more powerful, protest candidate: his platform was defined by hostility to Labour as the government responsible for the war and dissatisfaction with the 'official' opposition provided by the Conservatives and the Liberal Democrats. The same, indeed, is true of the Green Party's presentation of itself. In their introduction to the party's manifesto, Caroline Lucas MEP and Keith Taylor concentrated on underlining the difference between the Greens and 'the Westminster parties' by stressing realism, honesty and compassion in a manner that was deliberately designed to build on the lack of trust in mainstream political parties. Although the Greens never sold themselves as a party of protest, their platform was stridently presented in terms of being a 'real' alternative: a party that you could vote for if you were dissatisfied with all the major choices.

Despite its immediate appeal as a means of explaining the success of minor parties, however, the 'no party' phenomenon is not sufficient to describe the fortunes of all minority candidates. It models accurately the gains made by the Greens and is an adequate description of the fortunes of certain independents, such as Keys and Law, but it significantly fails to rationalise either the continued success of candidates such as Richard Taylor or the emergence of Respect and the BNP as major political forces. While the 'no party' model is a powerful method of understanding why a politically interested elector with broadly centrist attitudes would vote for the Greens as an act of protest, it does not provide any explanation of why some voters should have decided not only to participate in the electoral process, but also to give their support to a party or candidate far removed from the terms of political debate at Westminster. It is a good model of negative voting amongst disaffected centrists but is weak in that it fails to provide any insight into the positive reasons behind the determination of a vote. Put more simply, it can show why someone voted Green as a means of *not* voting Labour, Liberal Democrat or Conservative, but it cannot justify why someone should have voted *for* Respect or the BNP instead of simply not voting at all.

Push–pull: 'positive' voting and the specific failure model

Fewer people are voting than in the past and, what is more, fewer people are interested in politics. Although the turnout at the 2005 election was marginally higher than in 2001, the 61 per cent of the population who turned out to vote was still more than 10 points lower than at the 1997 election and 15 points lower than the average turnout between 1945 and 2001. This apathy is for many commentators the direct outcome of the convergence of the major parties and the stagnancy of political debate. In this sense, it is the counterpart of the 'no party' phenomenon. While some of the voters who are disenchanted with mainstream dialogue choose to display their frustration by casting a protest vote in a general election, others shrug their shoulders, stay at home and try to find something on television that doesn't involve politics.

Given that fewer people are interested enough in politics to vote, the problem is very much a matter of determining what space exists within conventional political dialogue to allow minor parties to instil into potentially apathetic voters a powerful positive reason to support them at an election. It is more than evident that if minority candidates are succeeding (in the sense either of winning a seat or of increasing their share of the vote) while voter apathy is strong, then at the same time as a selection of voters feel themselves to be alienated from the terms of mainstream politics, minor parties are successfully attracting their support by tapping into the weakness of their interest in what the Greens called 'Westminster politics'. This crucial political moment – the fulcrum about which the movement away from mainstream dialogue and towards minority candidacies occurs – is of central importance in explaining the success of many minor parties and, in turn, of illustrating the vacuum at the heart of debate within the major parties.

Modelling the success of parties such as the BNP, however, is not merely a matter of explaining why people should wish to vote for their candidates, but also of determining what in the terms or effects of mainstream political dialogue has created the opportunity or reason for the existence of that support. While there are certainly 'positive' reasons for individuals to vote for a BNP candidate, it is nevertheless the case that there are also particular reasons why that individual should have thought it necessary to look outside of the confines of tripartite Westminster politics. These latter reasons are, in every sense, inescapably representative of definitive failures at the heart of major-party debate and candidacies. Therefore the model that follows may be described either in terms of specific failures in mainstream politics (whether within a dialogue or as the consequence of actions emerging out of the parliamentary process) operating alongside 'positive' attractions of minority parties, or, rather more prosaically, as a matter of push (away from tripartite politics, but into a different area of political engagement) and pull (towards specific minority candidates).

With some minor parties and independent candidates, the essence of the push-pull dynamic is readily apprehensible. Richard Taylor's IKHHC programme, and his seizure and retention of the Wyre Forest seat, is an excellent initial example. From September 2000, IKHHC has campaigned on the basis of the health authority's failure to uphold its promise not to reduce the standard of service at Kidderminster Hospital, and has persistently demanded the institution of such basic facilities as local accident and emergency and intensive care units. In Taylor's case, it is evident that the specifically local problem of inadequate healthcare provision, which from 2000 has been associated with the Labour Party at a regional and a national level, stimulated the emergence of an electoral caucus that was prepared to support an independent candidate dedicated specifically to rectifying this want. From the electors' perspective, they were 'pushed' away from the Labour incumbent by the specific failure to uphold healthcare standards in Kidderminster, and then further 'pushed' away from mainstream dialogue by the inadequacy of Liberal Democrat and Conservative candidates at successive elections. On the other hand, they were 'pulled' towards Taylor by his distance from the contrivances of Westminster politicians and particularly by his commitment to raise local concerns as a local man in a national forum.

The specific failure of conventional dialogue in the case of Wyre Forest was extremely local. Central government – manifested as the health authority and represented until 2001 by a Labour MP – had failed to provide basic healthcare in a particular locality. It was held to be distant and unconcerned. Taylor's successive victories illustrate the

importance of the perceived distance between the apparently conver-
gent 'Westminster' parties and the actual problems of life in towns and
villages around Britain. In this sense, his election triumphs are the direct
corollary of the campaigning methods employed by other candidates
across the country. Jeremy Hunt (Conservative, South West Surrey),
has been mentioned in an earlier chapter because of the extraordinary
attention he paid to local issues in his constituency, but he is both
representative of a broader trend and, along with Taylor, a reflection of
the room created for alternative candidacies by the specific local failure
of mainstream political dialogue. The perceived preoccupation of the
major parties with appearance, spin and sound-bites has led to a feeling
amongst voters in constituencies such as Wyre Forest that they are
simply being 'ignored' or 'left out'. In Kidderminster the crisis faced by
the hospital merely brought this sense of alienation sharply into focus
and moved it towards the centre of the election campaign.

Although it does not immediately appear comparable, the success of
the UK Independence Party mirrors neatly the performance of
IKHHC. It is true that UKIP is not tied to a particular constituency or
locality in the same way as Taylor's campaign is, but that does not mean
that the policy issue on which it is based is not the subject of a specific
failure in mainstream dialogue or a matter of concern to a large and
growing number of people. Since Tony Blair's Labour Party came to
power in 1997, between 19 per cent and 30 per cent of voters have
mentioned the issue of Europe in MORI polls as being important to
their deciding which party to vote for. At the same time, between
33 per cent and 40 per cent of all people questioned in companion polls
have indicated that they believe none of the three major parties have the
best policy on this issue. Although not all the people who have
mentioned Europe as an important issue would regard it as the single
most significant one for them in determining the way they would
vote, and not all of these people would believe that none of the
Conservatives, Labour and the Liberal Democrats have an adequate
policy on this subject, it is nevertheless possible to conclude that there
is a sizeable number of people for whom Europe is indeed a highly
important political issue and for whom the major parties have failed to
provide an attractive policy. UKIP itself acknowledges that it exists and

that it succeeds because of the public's awareness of a specific political failure with respect to policy on the European Union. Indeed, the party's leader, Roger Knapman MEP, began his 'Forword' (*sic*) to the party's election manifesto with the statement: 'The UK Independence Party exists because none of the old political parties are prepared to accept that the real government of Britain is now in Brussels.' It is questionable why Europe should have assumed such importance to the British electorate, but given that it is perceived as a problem of notable significance, it is remarkable that the specific failure of the three major parties to break through the restraints of political convergence and to offer an attractive policy solution has created the political space for the emergence of a relatively forceful single-issue party such as UKIP and has given rise to the electoral dissatisfaction to allow for UKIP's acquisition of nearly 600,000 votes in 2005.

In the same way as the success of IKHHC and UKIP, the fortunes of Respect and the BNP may be explained extremely well by the push-pull model. Each of these parties propounded at the 2005 general election a programme which, while broad and comprehensive, was far removed from the terms of the political dialogue taking place within the framework of tripartite or 'Westminster' politics. Although the war against Iraq was the immediate catalyst for the formation of Respect, the party is committed to extreme left-wing policies which to the casual observer appear twenty or thirty years out of date. Its platform centred on providing 'an alternative to imperialist war, unfettered global capitalism, and the rule of the market' and advocated a programme of radical renationalisation in major service areas coupled with an internationalist, pacifist outlook. In a similarly removed fashion, the BNP stated in its manifesto that while it maintained its staunch opposition to multi-culturalism it also stood for 'a British national economy' and was 'opposed to globalism, international socialism, laissez-faire capitalism and economic liberalism'. Autarchy and trade restrictions were proposed as the hallmarks of economic policy while at the same time the introduction of a 'Bill of Rights' and the reinstitution of the right to bear arms were key to their social policy agenda. These proposals, along with those made by Respect, are sufficiently detached from the conventional terms of contemporary political debate that, even assuming a high level of voter ignorance, it is extremely difficult to explain entirely the success of these parties within the framework of a protest model of voting. Given the radicalism of the two programmes and the unpleasant nature of some policies, it is clear that there is something which exercises a very strong positive (or 'pulling') influence on the determination of voting in an age of mounting apathy. However, what this positive influence and, more importantly, what the corresponding failure of mainstream debate or government action could be is rather more difficult to establish than for IKHHC and UKIP, precisely because of the extreme nature of the parties concerned.

Considering the case of the BNP in isolation, it would be all too easy to give excessive credence to the superficial view of it as a viciously racist organisation. Simply to describe the push–pull mechanism in terms of the attitudes of a relatively small number of deluded, disaffected and distasteful electors is to offer an undemanding, but misleadingly crude and prejudicial, explanation of the party's success. It remains true that those who are drawn to the BNP because of its highly unpleasant undertones are operating on the basis of a particular view of ethnicity and hence perceive there to be a specific failure in addressing 'racial' questions. Yet this does not take account of either the party's recent efforts to broaden its purview and to make itself a more attractive political alternative or the fact that the growth of its support far outstrips the changes in attitude towards issues of immigration recorded in national polls.

Similarly, regarding Respect as an isolated political phenomenon, it would be extremely tempting to reject any interpretation of its success as the aggregate outcome of voters' rational support for far-left politics and to present its performance merely as the outcome of reaction to the Blair government's decision to invade Iraq and the perceived failure of the Conservatives and the Liberal Democrats to provide adequate opposition. Again, while it is true that massive public participation in demonstrations against the war – such as that which occurred in London on Saturday 19 March 2005 – indicate a large groundswell of disapproval, it is far from evident that Respect's successes can be ascribed purely to this cause. There are two significant points to contradict such a view. Firstly, there was in fact a great deal of political opposition to the war in Iraq from within Westminster. The Liberal Democrats prided themselves throughout the 2005 general election campaign on having resisted military action from the beginning and, as Chapter 4 showed, some strategists even complained that the party's anti-war credentials were overplayed. Respect was, therefore, not the only party to be vigorous in its opposition to the war in Iraq. Secondly – and more importantly – if Respect's success could be attributed largely to its anti-war stance, then it would have experienced little variation in the level of its support between constituencies. Indeed, the party might have been expected to perform with equal success in areas of radically different social and ethnic composition. To take one obvious example, if the anti-war explanation is true, then it would be reasonable to expect similar levels of support for Respect candidates in both, say, East Ham, in London, and Hove, on the south coast. In reality, however, Respect performed relatively badly in Hove, yet managed to capture 20.7 per cent of the vote in East Ham. The inescapable conclusion is that factors other than opposition to the war in Iraq – the level of which was fairly constant around Britain – were responsible for Respect's success.

In the case of both the BNP and Respect, it seems that it is too simplistic to explain the political moment of their success in terms of either racism or anti-war sentiments. Yet even if it is acknowledged that their programmes contain particular policies which may have resonance with some voters, it still remains true that their success appears to outstrip the accrual of support which might have been expected given national trends and the performance of related organisations in the past. There is, it appears, a missing quantity in the push–pull equation.

This missing quantity can be found in the similarities between the BNP and Respect. It is not merely the case that they are comparable political phenomena (in terms of success): they are the two sides of the same coin. That is not to say that there is anything equivalent in their world-views. Although they may happen to agree on certain issues (they both oppose globalisation, for example), their reasoning and their fundamental beliefs are a world apart. Rather it is the case that the demographics which support the successes of each party share a common sociological foundation and arise from the same political failure.

Respect is a fascinating study. Although it received the overwhelming majority of its publicity on account of the candidacy of a sturdy, white, Scottish member of Parliament, boasted frequently of its support from major trade unions and was proud of the backing it received from celebrities such as the film director Ken Loach, it openly acknowledged that it carved its electoral constituency using quite different tools. On 5 May 2005, it was not trade unionists nor disaffected Labour voters who turned out to support Respect candidates in their droves: rather it was an entirely new combination of ethnic-minority voters who swelled polling stations to back Respect. As Alan Thornett, a member of the party's steering committee, explained shortly after the general election, 'Respect's unique achievement was that it was able to break through both the electoral system and the stultifying election campaign, by building dynamic campaigns in key inner-city, traditional Labour, working-class constituencies with big immigrant communities – Muslim, but not only Muslim – which could concentrate a big vote.'[2]

Inner-city constituencies, largely populated by substantial Islamic communities, supported Respect candidates – often from the same religious background – on an unprecedented scale. Unlike any other political party, Respect successfully capitalised on previously unaligned demographic groups, a large number of whom had not even voted before. In many senses, it can be seen to have 'politicised' a number of Muslim communities.[3]

The positive ('pull') reasons for Muslim support for Respect seem to lie in the party's overt attempts to appeal to major areas of Islamic concern from the advantageous position of a political party with a real chance of success (unlike the Islam Zinda Baad Platform, whose sole candidate polled only 361 votes) but untainted by political history. The party's manifesto clearly stated its intention to combat the 'demonisation of Muslim communities' and to oppose in the strongest possible terms the likelihood that anti-terror legislation would lead to greater police surveillance of Muslim people. Similarly, it stressed the moral importance of community, which, while remaining true to many of the party members' socialist heritage, was freed from the constraints of political history and therefore able to coincide neatly with the communitarian and charitable aspects of Islamic belief. At a more practical level, it advocated giving unprecedented support to the lowest-paid workers, including those whose employment might not necessarily allow them access to union membership. As the conflict between British Airways and Gate Gourmet in the late summer of 2005 illustrated, it was frequently the case that those from ethnic minorities were most likely to suffer from poor working conditions and low wages.

As the positive reasons for Respect's success suggest, the specific failures of government and political discourse (the 'push' reasons) which assisted it are necessarily concerned primarily with the condition of Muslim communities. It is perfectly conventional to say that those who are entitled to vote from Muslim backgrounds had seldom done so until the advent of Respect candidacies. Yet what is so interesting about the party, and what is so significant for the wider condition of British politics, is the reason why so few Muslim voters had taken advantage of their electoral rights.

In a lecture given to the Manchester Council for Community Relations on 22 September 2005, Trevor Phillips, the chairman of the Commission for Racial Equality, warned that Britain was in danger of heading towards a future of racial segregation, characterised by 'passively co-existing ethnic and religious communities, eyeing each other uneasily over the fences of our differences'. At the heart of his warning was the contention that 'younger Britons appear to be integrating' into British society 'less well than their parents' and that no effort was being made to reverse the trend.

What is significant about Phillips's lecture is that he highlighted political failure as the reason for the unconscious imposition of artificial divisions between different ethnic or religious groups. It was not, he implied, that there was any intrinsic barrier to the integration of different groups within a rich, multi-cultural whole, but that there was a lack of political impetus behind any attempts to prevent migrant families 'steadily [drifting] away from the rest of us, evolving their own lifestyles, playing by their own rules'. Although he was rather vague about details, Phillips's point was absolutely valid. Despite the fact that a proportion of first- and second-generation migrant families, particularly those from Muslim backgrounds, have managed to live and thrive as full participants in British society, the overwhelming majority have not only been left on the social and economic margins of society, but passively ostracised and self-exiled from further participation in national and regional government.

At the heart of this is a massive political failure. Successive governments and opposition parties have signally failed to propose any method of reaching out more actively to Muslim communities in particular. They are left 'marooned outside the mainstream', as Phillips put it. Behind this is an intellectual failure. This failure is that of identity and philosophy. As Labour, the Conservatives and the Liberal Democrats have dashed for the perceived centre ground, there has been a reluctance to propound any notion of nation or concept of government. What Britain is, what it stands for and how it relates to different faiths and cultures are questions which, although suddenly forced to the centre stage of political debate after the 7 July bombs, were simply not answered. More importantly, the function of government with relation to communities and groups and its responsibility towards individuals and nation are issues which are completely neglected. Although it is more than evident that the emergence of a divided and even passively segregated society is the reason behind the highly restricted involvement of Muslim voters in the electoral process in the past and the cause of untold social and economic problems, there is a specific failure of the three major parties to put forward a theory of pluralistic government which might serve as the foundation for future political action.

This dearth of pluralistic thought is the source of the reasons which 'pushed' Muslim voters towards Respect at the 2005 general election and created the political room for an Islam-friendly leftist party to succeed. Yet, perhaps ironically, the problem of pluralism is also the cause of the BNP's increased success. It is the continued existence of the perception of a fragmented and disparate society, divided along ethnic and religious lines, which facilitates appeal of the less appetising aspects of the party's programme. More than this, however, it is the absence of a comprehensive and unifying theory of the national state and government, which could arouse conscious approbation amongst even the most varied communities, that creates the political space for the propagation of a radicalised but self-contained vision of Britain's future. The absence of such a theory allows not only for the continued attachment of significance to superficial ethnic and/or religious differences but also for the development of political ideologies which arise from the perception of distinction and which respond to the intellectual need for an explanation of national identity and the function of government. Put more simply, the death of ideology, in which all three of the major parties have been complicit, has allowed Respect and the BNP to succeed.

It is possible, indeed, to see the major parties' retreat from ideological approaches to nation and state not merely as the sociological and intellectual cause of the rise of the BNP and Respect, but also as the catalyst for the success of parties such as UKIP and the IKHHC. Earlier in this chapter, it was suggested that the successes of these two latter parties was due to the failure of conventional political dialogue to address specific issues. This remains absolutely true. The major parties' failure to deal adequately with the question of further integration with the European Union (evidenced by the sitting-on-the-fence approach of Gordon Brown's 'five tests') and local issues were the immediate causes of the rise of Richard Taylor and the national growth of UKIP's support. Yet this is only a partial explanation. The Labour government, the Conservatives and the Liberal Democrats have singularly failed to tackle local issues and the problem of Europe primarily because they have no fully developed and commonly agreed conception of the function of government. Without an awareness of the purpose of government, it is intellectually impossible to explain what obligations are owed by a central executive to local communities and extremely difficult to determine whether it is better to remain outside or to become a fuller part of a more closely interlinked Europe. Although he stopped short of admitting the theoretical complications arising from his party's lack of a philosophy of government and certainly did not confess to the confusion in policy that it has caused, Brown clearly indicated his awareness of New Labour's philosophical poverty. In a speech which was widely interpreted as being a bid for the leadership at the 2005 party conference, the Chancellor boldly said that, since 1997, Labour hadn't 'really been talking about *why* we're in government'. The function of government and the ends to which the governing party wished to put their authority were, he suggested, simply open questions for a party which had become obsessed with the retention of power. The way in which different racial and ethnic groups fitted within a broader whole and the manner in which individuals of every background related to an overarching and unifying set of ideas had, he implied, also been eschewed in the process.

Prospects, the poverty of philosophy and the crisis of pluralism

Under both the protest model and the push-pull model of voting, the minor parties' prospects are inescapably tied to the future behaviour of Labour, the Conservatives and the Liberal Democrats. Yet the fortunes of the candidates whose performance can best be explained by the protest model may very well turn out to be quite different to those of parties whose success is better conceived of in terms of the push-pull model. While the parties of protest, such as the Greens, are dependent on the perpetuation of the 'no party' phenomenon and a continuing ground-swell of disapproval, the parties that provide a 'positive' reason to potential supporters – such as the BNP and Respect – are reliant on the more subtle persistence of philosophical indifference in the major parties.

There is no doubt that protest voting increased in the period 1997–2005, but there is no clear indication that it will continue to do so. It is, after all, dependent not only on the status of mainstream political dialogue but also on the psychology of the individual protestor. As a consequence, there is some evidence to suggest that it will, in fact, begin to plateau. As voter apathy continues apace and the likelihood of a change of government in the imminent future seems remote, the urge to register protest may decline. If it continues, it is not unreasonable to suggest that alternative parties might well be considered more likely to register a higher impact at elections. In this way, it might be possible for a Green supporter to transfer their support to a Respect candidate in some areas under the belief that Respect may be better able to challenge a major-party candidate. As the parties of positive attraction receive publicity for greater-than-expected success at the 2005 general election, it may be that they appear a more attractive recipient of support amongst those who are intent on registering their protest at the content of mainstream dialogue. For the Greens, therefore, and for candidates such as Reg Keys and Peter Law, it seems more than likely that without a 'positive' attraction for the electorate and in the absence of a shocking development, their support will at best remain stable.

For the BNP, UKIP and Respect, however, the future seems altogether different. Their prospects are, above all else, reliant on the intellectual inertia of the New Politics. They depend for their success in future on the deepening of the divides in British society and the continuity of philosophical reluctance among the three major parties. Of these two, the more important is inevitably the possibility that none of the major parties will develop a clear conception of the function of government, the identity of the nation and the operation of a pluralistic society. It is this which will determine whether the divisions within communities and the gulf between individuals and government are further damaged or healed. In previous chapters, the condition of each of the Labour Party, the Conservatives and the Liberal Democrats was examined in detail and the fault-lines of debate considered in depth. These clearly demonstrated that, in the aftermath of the 2005 general election, each of the parties was struggling desperately with the political effects of the success of the New Politics and striving to achieve a new identity and a new direction. In essence, debate within each concerned the central questions of nation, state and government. The Conservatives were preoccupied with the relationship of the individual with government; the Labour Party was divided between corporatism and economic liberalism; and the Liberal Democrats were similarly rent asunder by the contradictions between liberal laissez-faire and the implications of social responsibility. Political debate within each of the three major parties was hence dominated by exactly the problems which had stimulated the rise of the BNP, Respect and UKIP. Yet, as previous chapters have shown, it is highly unlikely that any of the Conservatives, the Liberal Democrats or New Labour will be able to resolve their internal problems so as to deliver the clear philosophy of government which has been so conspicuously missing since 1997.

Given the fact that party politics is fundamentally the art of compromise, and given also the terrible contradictions which have simmered under the surface of each of the major parties, it is probable that for the sake of preserving unity, the critical relationship between individual, nation and government will be shelved in favour of a pragmatic adoption of commonly agreed policies. The fact that David Willetts was prepared to abandon his own ambitions to support David Davis in the Conservative leadership election is alone a demonstration of the primacy of party integrity over ideological belief.

Granted the perpetuation of the poverty of philosophy – and most particularly, the paucity of pluralistic thought – in mainstream political dialogue, it seems reasonable to suggest that the conditions which are favourable to the success of parties such as the BNP, UKIP and Respect will continue to improve, if one can use such a description. Without any clear ideological identity founded upon a definitive philosophy of government, there will be limited opportunity for any of the major parties represented in the House of Commons to provide measures to arrest the isolation of individuals from the group and the division of communities along social, economic and ethnic lines. Voting intentions are, in the absence of a clear delineation between the major parties, set to become more fluid and increasingly radicalised. Traditional patterns of voting may lose their integrity further and, while the composition of the Commons may change little, government may well become more distant from the electorate.

Of course, it is all too easy to speculate about the extent of the future success of the BNP, Respect and UKIP based on the internal politics of the 'Westminster' parties. Yet the fact remains that their success is more than likely to continue and grow. This is remarkable in its own right but, given that it will emerge as an outcome of the debates within the major parties, becomes all the more worthy of attention and concern. The performance of minority candidates at the 2005 general election is, above all else, an illustration and a symptom of the tremendous problems besetting British politics following the triumph of the New Politics. It is a demonstration of the importance of ideology and of the significance of a philosophy of nation and state, and a stark reminder of the tremendous, pragmatic inertia which obstructs the reinvigoration of mainstream political debate. Most pertinently, it indicates dramatically the overriding intellectual, electoral and sociological need for a fresh consideration of the philosophical foundations of government.

Conclusion

I predict a riot . . .

Ten years after the release of Mathieu Kassovitz's film *La Haine*, France was convulsed by riots. Beginning with disturbances in Clichy-sous-Bois which followed the deaths of Zyed Benna and Bouna Traore during a police chase on 27 October 2005, violence fanned out across the country. For almost three weeks, the dark suburbs of Paris, Lille, Bordeaux, Lyons and a dozen other cities were lit by the flames of burning cars and filled with the sound of street fighting, glass shattering and police sirens. The situation was worst in the *banlieues*, the huge, purpose-built concrete suburbs populated by the poorest elements of French society and home to the large north African émigré communities from which Zyed and Bouna had come. In these areas, the vast, featureless tower blocks, each of which could tell its own unique version of the depressingly familiar tale of deprivation and squalor, looked down on vicious pitched battles between multi-ethnic cohorts of disaffected youths and heavily armed lines of police. Shots were fired, rocks thrown, vehicles overturned and buildings set on fire. Shops were looted indiscriminately and property worth millions of euros was destroyed where the economic damage could be sustained least. After seven days the rioting seemed to have acquired its own momentum and for a brief period it appeared as if nothing could stop the carnage.

The tragic circumstances of Zyed and Bouna's death were emblematic of *la crise des banlieues* and it is not difficult to see why their demise proved to be such a powerful rallying point for so many people. Two north African immigrants living in a run-down suburb of the French capital, they suffered the extremes of first-world poverty. Unable to enjoy the security of a stable and sufficient income, possessed of very little education, and with almost nothing to do, they turned to crime. It was perhaps inevitable that they should finally have run into the police. Chased through the back streets of Clichy-sous-Bois by gendarmes, they dived into an electrical substation. Before they could even catch their breath, they were electrocuted. To those who lived in similar circumstances in the forgotten world of the *banlieues*, where poverty is a way of life, where crime is almost ritualised and where state authorities are either a distant memory or an occasional and despised source of trouble, Zyed and Bouna's death seemed to be an encapsulation of their lives and a bitter reminder of the frustration they endured.

There is no doubt that the riots of late October and early November 2005 were the result of deep-rooted social and political problems. Appalling living standards, high levels of crime, poor education and the failure to integrate disparate and desperate immigrant groups into French society certainly played their role both in Zyed and Bouna's death and also in the horrific violence which followed. So too did the palpable mistrust of and hostility towards the police as an organ of government contribute to the outbreak of the riots and obstruct their successful suppression.

What is most troubling about these problems, however, is the fact that they were evident in France at least ten years previously. After the shooting by police in February 1993 of Makomé M'Bowole, a Zairean immigrant, the riots which ensued illustrated clearly the social afflictions and political divisions within French society. French politicians were certainly not unaware of the condition of many people, particularly in *banlieues*. Indeed, the M'Bowole riots so haunted the Prime Minister, Alain Juppé, that he requested a private screening for his Cabinet of *La Haine*, which vividly depicted suburban deprivation in the wake of the violence, on its release two years later.

Yet despite the fact that Cabinet ministers were shocked and appalled at what they had seen reflected in Kassovitz's film, little attempt was made to change the terms of conventional political discourse to rectify the situation. For the next ten years, mainstream French politics consistently failed to address social issues. Living standards, social identity, ethnic integration and popular association with government organs were, but for the occasional rhetorical remark for the cameras, ignored. Indeed, it was almost as if the fundamentally social dimension of politics had been forgotten.

Despite France's long history of social communitarianism, in the twelve years between the shooting of Makomé M'Bowole and the death of Zyed Benna and Bouna Traore the dialogues of French politics had become less and less attached to the 'social' as a positive sphere of human action. Economic liberalism and an attachment to free markets came to dominate in the thought of politicians, who more and more overtly considered themselves to be managers. The towering figures of late twentieth-century French politics, such as François Mitterrand, with their still strong belief in the great ideologies had become at best anachronistic ghosts and at worst forgotten follies. Politicians such as Nicolas Sarkozy – likened by many commentators to Tony Blair – seemed gradually to become dominant, not by force of argument or thought but by following the path of least resistance, as any good manager would wish. While this shift in political manner from Mitterrand to Sarkozy may well have been an eminently sensible development in a more 'capitalist' and free-market world, less dominated by the great wars of ideology than in the past, the effect of abandoning the social dimension of politics has been devastating. As the riots of late October and early November 2005 demonstrate, social problems and social unrest, far from diminishing, have become worse. Living standards in the *banlieues* are as bad as they ever were; crime and drug addiction is more widespread; racial tension is higher than ever; and the dislocation (in both senses) of people from politics is more pronounced. The frustration that this has generated – that great ground-swell of resentment – has grown to new and more violent proportions. Moreover, at the same time as the inhabitants of the *banlieues* are feeling ever more distant from the content of mainstream political dialogue, a growing number of French people are finding common cause with more radical elements. As Jean-Marie Le Pen's 2002 presidential candidacy alone demonstrates, far-right politics is on the rise and the increase in its support shows no signs of dissipating. If, therefore, the period 1995–2005 could be characterised as the new age of Sarkozy, it could be described with no less meaning as the age of Le Pen – the age of privation, division and hatred.

While the French experience of social unrest and political radicalisation seems extreme, it is Anglo-Saxon hubris to imagine that France is unique. In successive chapters, this book has demonstrated that the British public, like their French counterparts, are associating themselves less and less closely with the terms of conventional political dialogue. The discourse of economic liberalism, individualism and anti-communitarianism, engendered by the growth of a managerialist approach to politics within New Labour, may have revolutionised Westminster politics, but it has alienated a great number of British voters, particularly in those regions where living standards are lowest, crime is highest and racial tension is rising. Although each of the three major parties contains elements which have recognised the need for social concern and a renewed belief in the benefit of collective action and identity, they remain minority elements readily eclipsed by the post-Thatcherite managerial majority. Faced with parties which are unwilling to address the very real requirement for at least a degree of communitarian thought, a growing number of British voters are turning to the extreme fringes of politics. More and more people are becoming radicalised and at the same time more politicised. At the same time as the British National Party has mobilised considerable support for its racially intolerant programme, Respect has taken advantage of the failure to integrate minority communities into a broader social whole and emerged as a threatening new force in British politics. The French riots may have been more violent and widespread, and the success of Le Pen more pronounced than anything yet witnessed in Britain, but nevertheless, the experience of France remains a poignant warning of what may be yet to come.

It is clear that if Britain is to stem the tide of public dissociation from politics and avert the potential crisis of radicalism, change is necessary. The burden of change, however, falls on precisely those bodies whose reluctance to deviate from the path of managerialism has brought politics to this unfortunate juncture. The voices of social concern within each of the three major parties have been lost among the tumultuous cries of the anti-ideological, managerialist rabble and there is no indication that the situation will alter. Even though the 2005 general election demonstrated that Labour, the Conservatives and the

Liberal Democrats each need to re-evaluate their political programmes in the face of a volatile electorate whose sympathy for spin and triangulation has expired, not one seems willing to do so in a serious manner. Although Gordon Brown is likely to succeed to the leadership of the Labour Party in the near future and his 2005 conference speech seemed to indicate some room for hope, his approach to reform of the pensions system demonstrates that he is no longer the mast to which the colours of communitarianism may be hung.[1] Similarly, the struggle for the Conservative leadership between David Davis and David Cameron, each of whom is a 'Soho' moderniser, illustrates the extent to which the party is unwilling to consider the social paternalism earlier advocated so lucidly by David Willetts. At the same time, although the Liberal Democrats retain some continuing affection for social democracy, the divisions within the party are sufficiently severe that any serious effort to move further in this direction is likely to catalyse a civil war of a scale which would make even the Conservative Party baulk.

Within the three major parties, therefore, there is in fact a burgeoning element of social concern and of a communitarian approach. There are those, some well placed and highly respected, who do believe that government can and should perform a valuable social function, that collective action can be a force for good and that, in many cases, corporative action is needed to prevent the worsening of already present social problems. The problem is, however, that these community-minded individuals and groups are swamped by the structure of Westminster politics. It could be argued that Britain actually has a subtle form of two-party politics – divided between the economic liberals and the communitarians – but that its potential has been curtailed by the fact that it exists within the framework of three-party politics. The dash away from ideology and the desperate dash towards the 'middle ground' that the New Politics stimulated has inhibited all of the three major parties considering at all seriously the communitarian and socially paternalistic views of some of their number.

To a very large extent, what has prevented the social dimension of politics from receiving closer consideration from the major parties is the reluctance of communitarian-minded figures to make their views heard more loudly. The few speeches that have been made have been delivered to small, select groups behind closed doors and publications making the case for the profoundly social function of government have been deliberately circulated to a small readership. While there is no doubt that there is a latent discourse of this social function, it requires not only a fuller and more detailed elucidation from its timid adherents but also a concerted effort to bring it into public policy debates.

In the introduction to the 1938 edition of his book *A Grammar of Politics*, Harold Laski wrote:

> Our age . . . is an age of critical transition in which, as at the end of the fifteenth and eighteenth centuries, a new social order is struggling grimly to be born. Our scheme of values is in the melting pot, and the principles of its refashioning have not yet been determined. As always, in such a time, men have gone back to the foundations of politics; and they seek anew to explain the nature and functions of the state. There is a confusion in the atmosphere of discussion which betokens the advent of a revolutionary age.

Laski's words, intended to apply to a world caught between liberal capitalism, fascism and communism, are no less valid for Britain today than they were when first written. Facing challenges more subtle, yet perhaps no less frightening, in their scope and potential, the politics of Britain – the dialogue of which is ridden with the confusion that comes from an absence of firm principles – must return to their foundations for new direction.

No less than in any other age, men and women in Britain today find themselves living in communities, side by side with other human beings in a manner which could not but be considered social. As at any other time, man remains by some impulse, by some natural urge or force of habituated artifice, compelled to live as a social animal. This social setting requires a reason of organisation, a sense of collective identity and a notion of collective purpose with which all have association. The social environment, however, is not static; it is subject, like anything else that lives and breathes, that resides in the hearts and bodies of men and women, to the rule of constant evolution and development. As it changes, with altering mores and fluctuating composition, so too must conceptions of the social whole alter. Notions of social identity, of the collective, of the function of government, must be considered anew and adapted to these developments or else, through the cowardice of those to whom the whole has been entrusted, risk privation, hatred, violence and suffering of a scale and import greater than ever experienced in France. To paraphrase Henry Nevinson, society and government are things which we have to conquer afresh for ourselves every day, like love; after each victory we think we can settle down and enjoy it without further struggle, but the battle is never done, and the field of conflict is never quiet.[2]

Further reading

Chapter 1

David Butler and Dennis Kavanagh continue to produce the most useful and reliable works of reference for the general elections in question. In particular, see *The British General Election of 2005* (Basingstoke: Palgrave Macmillan, 2005), *The British General Election of 2001* (Basingstoke: Palgrave, 2001) and *The British General Election of 1997* (Basingstoke: Macmillan Press, 1997). For further and more lively discussions, see in particular Robert Worcester, Roger Mortimore and Paul Baines, *Explaining Labour's Landslip: The 2005 General Election* (London: Politico's, 2005) and Andrew Geddes and Jonathan Tonge (eds), *Labour's Second Landslide: The British General Election 2001* (Manchester: Manchester University Press, 2002). For additional data, consult MORI's excellent website: http://www.mori.com.

Electoral behaviour, and particularly the question of tactical voting, is the subject of considerable academic discussion and, as a consequence, little of the literature is accessible to the non-specialist. However, for a useful introduction to the major themes in this subject, see R. Niemi, G. Whitten, and M. Franklin, 'Constituency Characteristics, Individual Characteristics and Tactical Voting in the 1987 British General Election', *British Journal of Political Science* (1992), vol. 22, no. 2, pp. 229–240; G. Evans and A. Heath, 'A Tactical Error in the Analysis of Tactical Voting: A Response to Niemi, Whitten and Franklin', *British Journal of Political Science* (1993), vol. 23, no. 1, pp. 131–137; G. Evans and A. Heath, 'Tactical Voting: Concepts, Measurements and Findings', *British Journal of Political Science* (1994), vol. 24, no. 4 pp. 557–561. Lengthier treatments of the same subject can be found in, for example, David Denver and Gordon Hands, *British Electoral Behaviour: Voting and Volatility*, (London: I. B. Tauris, 1997) and in the more technical Thomas C. Schelling, *Micromotives and Macrobehaviour*, (New York: W. W. Norton, 1978). It is worth stating that there has been a marked paucity of investigation into the extent and effects of tactical voting and electoral fluidity since the 1997 general election and further study into this subject would be most helpful for understanding the apparent collapse of Labour's traditional social constituency.

Chapter 2

There is a striking dearth of literature on the New Labour governments. The years since 1997 have beckoned forth a rash of books seeking to define New Labour as a political project rather than a coherent theory of government or concrete philosophy. Frequently these sought to compare it with 'Old' Labour. Perhaps accurately reflecting its reputation, many studies addressed Blairism as an electoral machine, preferring, like Nicholas Jones's *Sultans of Spin: the Media and the New Labour Government* (London: Victor Gollancz, 1999), to debate how New Labour sells itself, rather than what it does in government and why. But most books focused upon either debating New Labour's break with its recent past (Steven Fielding, *The Labour Party: Continuity and Change in the Making of 'New' Labour* (Basingstoke: Palgrave, 2003)) or its adherence to an apparently unshaken Thatcherite consensus (Richard Heffernan, *New Labour and Thatcherism: Political Change in Britain* (Basingstoke: Macmillan Press, 2000)). The question upon which most chose to focus, then, is just how new New Labour really is. Good texts that chart the arrival of New Labour in No. 10 include Philip Gould, *The Unfinished Revolution: How the Modernisers Saved the Labour Party* (London: Little, Brown, 1998); Anthony Heath, Roger Jowell and John Curtice (eds), *Labour's Last Chance?: The 1992 Election and Beyond* (Aldershot: Dartmouth, 1994); and Peter Riddell's excellent essay 'The End of Clause IV, 1994-95', *Contemporary British History* (1997), vol. 11. Occasionally in the chapter I have quoted from Tony Blair, *New Britain: My Vision of a Young Country* (London, Fourth Estate,

1996), a good collection of his early speeches. All of Labour's manifestos from 1945 can be found on the Univeristy of Keele's website: http://www.psr.keele.ac.uk.

However, in-depth critiques of the Blair governments have been few and far between. Those which have caught the public's imagination have come from Cabinet quitters and the recently sacked, notably Clare Short, *An Honourable Deception?: New Labour, Iraq and the Misuse of Power* (London: Free Press, 2004) and Robin Cook, *The Point of Departure* (London: Simon and Schuster, 2003). But most of the attention has remained either on New Labour's relationship with the media or else on decision making during the Iraq War. This is highly significant and indicates either that there is very little worth saying about Blairism in office or that it has so far defied definition. Doubtless this situation will change when the Prime Minister steps down, but until then the literature on New Labour in office remains pre-millennium.

There are several outstanding histories of the Labour movement available. Among them can be counted Steven Fielding (ed.), *The Labour Party: Socialism and Society since 1951* (Manchester: Manchester University Press, 1997); and, for a more concise introduction, Kenneth O. Morgan, *Labour People: Leaders and Lieutenants, Hardie to Kinnock*, rev. edn (Oxford: Oxford University Press, 1992). The critical period for understanding the roots of triangulation is the 1970s and 1980s. Particularly good studies on Labour's development in this era can be found in Martin Holmes, *The Labour Government 1974–79: Political Aims and Economic Reality* (London: Macmillan, 1985); and David and Maurice Kogan, *The Battle for the Labour Party*, 2nd edn (London: Kogan Page, 1983). The standard volume on Labour–union relations remains Lewis Minkin, *The Contentious Alliance: Trade Unions and the Labour Party* (Edinburgh: Edinburgh University Press, 1991). Again Minkin's work is somewhat dated, stopping as it does at the point where the unions seemed to have become happy partners in reform with Neil Kinnock and his proto-New Labour agenda. It is telling that no similar study of New Labour's industrial relations is extant. Finally, history is written far too often by the winners and, for a glimpse of what might have been, read David Coates's analysis of Labour's years of conflict in

Labour in Power?: A Study of the Labour Government, 1974–1979 (London: Longman, 1980).

The transatlantic context of the Labour Party's triangulation has enjoyed a fair amount of comment and study. One of the most compelling assessments is Steven M. Gillon, *The Democrats' Dilemma: Walter F. Mondale and the Liberal Legacy* (New York: Columbia University Press, 1992), which charts the death of American social democracy. Two good accounts of what replaced it are Bill Clinton, *My Life* (New York: Alfred A. Knopf, 2004); and Stanley B. Greenberg and Theda Skocpol, *The New Majority: Toward a Popular Progressive Politics* (New Haven, CT and London: Yale University Press, 1997), a sympathetic reading of triangulation from two liberal historians. Arguably the critique that remains the most powerful explanation of what went wrong with the American left is Theodore J. Lowi, *The End of Liberalism: The Second Republic of the United States*, 2nd edn (New York: W. W. Norton, 1979). Richard M. Scammon and Ben J. Wattenberg's *The Real Majority* (New York: Coward-McCann, 1971) has dated, but makes its universal argument well that an emphasis upon 'social' issues can dramatically tip the electoral balance to the right.

Chapter 3

There is a wealth of literature on the Conservative Party, but it must be stated that not all of it is as valuable as it first appears. There are a great many memoirs and biographies available written by and about key figures, and although some, such as Sir Ian Gilmour's examination of Conservative thought from 1945 until the fall of Margaret Thatcher (*Dancing with Dogma: Britain under Thatcherism* (London: Simon and Schuster, 1992)), are extremely interesting, they should as a general rule be treated with some caution. Similarly, the party's chequered history since 1997 has given rise to very many historical and pseudo-historical surveys, a sizeable portion of which are to be avoided by those seeking to gain an impression of the politics of the years in opposition. Nevertheless, a number of works have appeared in recent years which are worthwhile points of reference. Anthony Seldon and Peter

Snowdon's *The Conservative Party: An Illustrated History* (Stroud: Sutton, 2004) and Geoffrey Wheatcroft's highly readable *The Strange Death of Tory England* (London: Allen Lane, 2005) are two recent books which have a broad enough scope and a sufficiently sophisticated edge to be used as reliable introductions to the major events and developments since 1997 and before. More detailed studies are somewhat harder to find, but the period 1997–2001 is well covered by two texts in particular. Simon Walters's *Tory Wars: Conservatives in Crisis* (London: Politico's, 2001) provides a detailed examination of the 2001 leadership election, while Mark Garnett and Philip Lynch's more recent book of essays, *The Conservatives in Crisis* (Manchester: Manchester University Press, 2003), is a fascinating treatment of key themes. In the latter, the chapters by Garnett on William Hague's leadership (pp. 49–65) and on the party's relationship with ideology (pp. 107–124) are particularly useful. Apart from Garnett's chapters, there is no satisfactory study of the party's struggle with its intellectual identity since 1997, but E. H. H. Green's *Ideologies of Conservatism: Conservative Political Ideas in the Twentieth Century* (Oxford: Oxford University Press, 2002) is an excellent and scholarly history of Conservative thought across a wider period.

Perhaps the most useful sources of information for the details of the debates regarding the future direction of the party are the speeches and articles of key figures, and it is extremely convenient that many of these may readily be found on a number of well-constructed websites. Think-tanks such as Iain Duncan Smith's Centre for Social Justice (http://www.centreforsocialjustice.org.uk) and the more right-leaning Centre for Policy Studies (http://www.cps.org.uk) also maintain excellent website archives. The speeches and articles preserved on the websites of MPs and think-tanks have proved to be invaluable in the writing of this chapter and it is to be hoped that effort will soon be put into assembling printed collections of these. As well as there being speeches given to interest groups and articles written for newspapers and magazines, it is fortunate for anyone wishing to study the party's recent intellectual trends that there have been a series of essay collections published since 1997. Since the collapse of Hague's 'leadership gamble' (as Garnett has described it) in 2001, there has indeed been something of an explosion in the number of collections written by Conservative thinkers. Of particular use is Sam Gyimah (ed.), *From the Ashes . . .: The Future of the Conservative Party* (London: Politico's, 2005), which was prepared specifically for the party conference season and includes essays by Ken Clarke, David Davis, David Cameron, Theresa May, Sir Malcolm Rifkind, David Willetts and numerous other key figures in recent Conservative history. Of similar value is Gary Streeter (ed.), *There is Such a Thing as Society: Twelve Principles of Compassionate Conservatism*, (London: Politico's, 2002), which reflects the beginnings of the Easterhouse modernisers well. See also the Soho-style essays in Edward Vaizey, Michael Gove and Nicholas Boles (eds), *A Blue Tomorrow: New Visions from Modern Conservatives* (London: Politico's, 2001).

Chapter 4

The contemporary Liberal Democratic Party has thus far avoided pronounced, objective academic study. A few, largely validatory, recent books include Roy Douglas, *Liberals: A History of the Liberal and Liberal Democratic Parties* (London: Hambledon and London, 2005); and Richard Bellamy, *Rethinking Liberalism* (London: Continuum, 2000). There is an abundance of literature on the New Liberalism of the early twentieth century, its rise, its fall and its intellectual trajectory. Some of the best amongst these are G. R. Searle, *The Liberal Party: Triumph and Disintegration, 1886–1929*, 2nd edn (Basingstoke: Palgrave, 2001); Michael Bentley, *The Climax of Liberal Politics: British Liberalism in Theory and Practice, 1868–1918* (London: Edward Arnold, 1987); and J. R. Hay, *The Origins of Liberal Welfare Reforms* (London: Macmillan, 1975). The Liberal Party's period of pronounced decline is little discussed but for an excellent biography of Jo Grimond (Michael McManus, *Jo Grimond: Towards the Sound of Gunfire* (Edinburgh: Birlinn, 2001)). The narrative of the SDP has attracted considerable attention and the story of the brief period of Social Democratic ascendancy has been often told, most notably in Ivor Crewe and Anthony King, *SDP: Birth, Life and Death of the Social Democratic Party* (Oxford: Oxford University Press, 1995). This details effectively the political implosion of British Social Democracy in the late 1980s, neatly exposing its tumultuous and frequently unwelcome deal with Liberalism. Of particular interest is its narration of the death of the Continuing SDP under David Owen's idiosyncratic, almost 'Neo-Thatcherite' leadership. For a summation of how some significant Social Democrats perceive themselves one might view Shirley Williams, *Politics is for People* (London: Allen Lane, 1981) and David Owen, *Time to Declare* (London: Michael Joseph, 1992), while Paddy Ashdown's autobiography (*The Ashdown Diaries*, 2 vols (London: Allen Lane, 2000–2001)) is a good introduction to modern Liberal experience. In the same political category as the latter is Paul Marshall and David Laws (eds), *The Orange Book: Reclaiming Liberalism* (London: Profile, 2004). Although this is a controversial publication it is also one of very few books to detail 'alternative' politics in a straightforwardly 'liberal' context.

For the wider issue of the New Politics and the rise of third parties one would do well to begin with comparative literature on US politics. Worth study is Stanley Greenberg, *Middle Class Dreams: The Politics and Power of the New American Majority*, rev. edn (New Haven, CT: Yale University Press, 1996), which argues that Ross Perot's two remarkable campaigns for the presidency were the product of similar forces that elected Bill Clinton, whilst also reflecting deep economic and political frustration on the part of the American electorate. It is also worth browsing through Frank Smallwood's *The Other Candidates: Third Parties in Presidential Elections* (Hanover, NH: University Press of New England, 1983) to understand the Anderson phenomenon of 1980.

Chapter 5

Partly as a result of what has – until recently – been a relatively poor showing at the polls, minor parties and independent candidatures have received minimal scholarly attention as a feature of contemporary British politics. There is, for example, no comprehensive single work dealing with minor parties and independent candidates for any part of the period dealt with in this book. The search for further reading of an authoritative nature is therefore frustrating, particularly when a general overview is desired. As a result, it is appropriate to mention only the most relevant works on specific minor parties.

The British National Party, despite being one of the more interesting electoral phenomena of recent years, has received little direct attention, perhaps as a consequence of their rather unsavoury programme, but it is still possible to find much that is of use in the literature dealing with the development of nationalist ideologies in a modern political environment. A fascinating general study of nationalist movements and the application of pluralistic ideas to their emergence is found in J. G. Kellas, *The Politics of Nationalism and Ethnicity*, 2nd edn (Basingstoke: Macmillan Press, 1998), and this should arguably be the first point of call. One of the rare cases of a serious inquiry into the resurgence of nationalism in Britain and its relationship to the BNP's fortunes is A. Heath, B. Taylor, L. Brook and A. Park, 'British National Sentiment,' *British Journal of Political Science* (1999), vol. 29, no. 1, pp. 155–175. Also of serious interest are Paul Hainsworth (ed.), *The Politics of the Extreme Right: From the Margins to the Mainstream* (London: Continuum, 2000) and Piero Ignazi, *Extreme Right Parties in Western Europe* (Oxford: Oxford University Press, 2003).

The Green Party, despite being one of the more established minor parties of British politics, is the subject of no single serious study. For an indication of its attempt to build its strategy around opposition to 'Westminster' parties, see the party's website, www.greenparty.org.uk, and its manifesto for the 2005 general election in particular. For a more detailed treatment of its performance at general elections, see the relevant chapters in Butler and Kavanagh's studies.

Respect, like Veritas and UKIP, is perhaps still too young to have received the detailed treatment it deserves. For the best available treatment, see Butler and Kavanagh's treatment of 'other parties' in their studies of the 1997, 2001 and 2005 general elections. There is also some useful information in Simon Henig and Lewis Baston, *Politico's Guide to the General Election 2005* (London: Politico's, 2005).

There is growing academic interest in the political position of minority communities and the problem of pluralism, but it is unfortunate that the attention given to the voting behaviour of Muslim communities, in particular, has not been examined in sufficient detail as yet. Useful studies of ethnic minorities, identity and politics in Britain include Shamit Saggar, *Race and Representation: Electoral Politics and Ethnic Pluralism in Britain* (Manchester: Manchester University Press, 2000); Philip Lewis, *Islamic Britain: Religion, Politics and Identity among British Muslims*, 2nd edn (London: I. B. Tauris, 2002); Tariq Modood, *Multicultural Politics: Racism, Ethnicity and Muslims in Britain* (Edinburgh: Edinburgh University Press, 2005); and Joel S. Fetzer and J. Christopher Soper, *Muslims and the State in Britain, France and Germany* (Cambridge: Cambridge University Press, 2005).

Notes

Chapter 1

1. In 2005, the metropolitan district of Liverpool, which is largely covered by Liverpool Riverside, was still ranked the most deprived local authority in Britain by National Statistics.
2. In 2005, the metropolitan district of Sheffield was ranked sixtieth of 354 local authorities with respect to deprivation according to National Statistics, where the first-placed authority is the most deprived area in Britain and 354th the least deprived.
3. Burnley was, in 2005, the thirty-seventh most deprived local authority in England.
4. C. Beale and I. Townsend, 'Unemployment by constituency, May 2005,' House of Commons Library Research Paper 05/47 (15 June 2005).
5. This deprivation ranking is for Tower Hamlets, which is roughly commensurate with Poplar & Canning Town.
6. It should be noted that this cannot be countered with any suggestion of tactical voting. If one performs a similar statistical analysis of swing away from Labour (relative to 2001) against 2001 majority, there is no evidence to suggest any kind of relationship.
7. D. Butler and D. Kavanagh, *The British General Election of 1992* (London: Macmillan, 1992), p. 231.
8. P.Cowley and M. Stuart, *Dissension amongst the Parliamentary Labour Party, 2001–2005: A Data Handbook* (produced in co-operation with the Economic and Social Research Council, the University of Nottingham and www.revolts.co.uk, 2005). See http://www.revolts.co.uk/dissensionamongsttheplp.pdf.

Chapter 2

1. Andrew Coulson, 'The Death of a Mass Membership Party?', *Renewal* (2005), vol. 13, no. 2/3.

2.   Bill Clinton, *My Life* (New York: Alfred A. Knopf, 2004).
3.   Clare Short, *An Honourable Deception?: New Labour, Iraq and the Misuse of Power* (London: Free Press, 2004).
4.   Alan Milburn, *Guardian*, 15 January 2005.

Chapter 3

1.   In late July 2005, the nine figures who had indicated a willingness to run for the leadership were (in alphabetical order) David Cameron, Kenneth Clarke, David Davis, Liam Fox, Andrew Lansley, Theresa May, Sir Malcolm Rifkind, David Willetts and Tim Yeo. At the party conference, five remained to give speeches: Cameron, Clarke, Davis, Fox and Rifkind. At this stage, Edward Leigh MP was considering standing as well. Shortly after giving his conference speech, Rifkind withdrew his candidacy to back Clarke.
2.   David Davis, 'Modern Conservatism', speech to Centre for Policy Studies, 4 July 2005.
3.   Ibid.
4.   Bernard Jenkin, 'To Be a Conservative: Changing the Conservative Party to Meet the Challenges of the 21st Century', speech to Policy Exchange, 19 July 2005.
5.   For details of Rifkind's remarks on announcing his intention to stand for the Conservative leadership, visit http://news.bbc.co.uk/1/hi/uk_politics/4617379.stm. For the later attempt to assume the mantle of a One Nation Conservative, see Sir Malcolm Rifkind, 'Building One Nation', speech to Conservative Mainstream, 15 September 2005.
6.   For a full text of these 'beliefs', visit http://www.conservatives.com/tile.do?def=party.beliefs.page.

Chapter 4

1.   Quoted in Giles Radice, *Friends and Rivals* (London: Little, Brown, 2002).

Chapter 5

1.   Those who defined themselves merely as 'Independents' are excluded, as are Scottish, Welsh and Northern Irish parties, which for these purposes are treated as major parties in their respective regions.

2.   Alan Thornett, quoted in Andy Newman, 'Respect's Big Opportunity', *Frontline* (2005), no. 17.

3.   By contrast, the party did not fare particularly well in those constituencies which have very small Muslim populations, such as Hove.

Conclusion

1.   It is worth noting that plans to reduce the role of unions in the determination of Labour Party policy further support the contention that the party is unwilling to return to its roots in social democracy and communitarianism. Under plans announced in the autumn of 2005, the unions would be allocated block votes amounting to 15 per cent of the party's total, giving them less than a third of the collective influence they had previously enjoyed.

2.   Nevinson's original remarks concerned freedom, the central issue of its day. The actual quotation is: 'For freedom, we know, is a thing that we have to conquer afresh for ourselves, every day, like love; and we are always losing freedom, just as we are always losing love, because, after each victory, we think we can now settle down and enjoy it without further struggle . . . The battle of freedom is never done, and the field is never quiet.' Nevinson, *Essays in Freedom* (London: Duckworth, 1909), p. xvi.

Index